family field guide

— SERIES —

VOLUME FOUR

Rocky Mountain Bugs

Insects and other Crawly Things

written by
Garrick Pfaffmann

illustrated by
Hilary Forsyth

BearBop Press LLC

BASALT COLORADO USA

© 2009 all rights reserved
printed in China

family field guide
— SERIES —

field notes

family field guide

family field guide

— S E R I E S —

field notes

ISBN-13: 9781882426324

Published by:

BearBop Press, LLC
www.bearboppress.com

Illustrated by:

Hilary Forsyth

Designed by:

words pictures colours graphic design

Distributed by:

Books West
www.bookswest.com

Library of Congress Control Number: 2009920439

Acknowledgements

Thanks to the many people who helped to ensure the accuracy of this book, especially to Dr. Boris Kondratieff of Colorado State University Entomology Department for editing. Also thanks to Lindsay, Judi Forsyth and Anne Siewert for their editing help. Special thanks to John, Mason and Bo for their patience. Thanks to the naturalists in my life who have taught me to look, question, research, and explore, especially Dale Abrams, Jim Kravitz, Gerrit Vynn and Jim Campbell.

Author's Dedication

In ecosystems,
as in human relationships,
give credit to the small things;
they are more important than we often realize,
and are too often overlooked and forgotten.

Illustrator's Dedication

For artists young and old
look closely at nature and it will unfold.
Patterns and colors on bugs delight
your eyes on each and every sight.

Quick Identification

Backswimmer p. 18

Caddisfly larva p. 20

Damselfly p. 22

Dragonfly p. 22

Mayfly nymph p. 24

Mosquito p. 26

Scud p. 28

Stonefly nymph p. 30

Water Boatman p. 32

Water Strider p. 34

Whirligig Beetle p. 36

Ant p. 38

Centipede p. 40

Cricket p. 42

Daddy Longlegs p. 44

family field guide

Earthworm p. 46

Earwig p. 48

Millipede p. 50

Roly-poly (pillbug) p. 52

Spider p. 54

Grasshopper p. 58

Ladybug p. 60

Slug p. 62

Spittlebug nymph p. 64

Tent Caterpillar p. 66

Tick p. 68

Bee p. 70

Butterfly p. 72-81

Moth p. 82

Wasp p. 84

family field guide

Introduction

WHY WATCH INSECTS AND OTHER BUGS?

To begin, the term *bug* in this book is a general term for any insect or similarly crawling, flying or wiggling invertebrate. Children love to watch, chase, catch and explore the world of insects and other bugs because they are easy to find, unique in shape, color and design, exciting to catch and, even for those afraid to touch these squirmy or flighty animals, most pose little threat of danger.

EASY TO FIND

Bugs are everywhere. Parents and teachers can easily guide kids to find bugs with little or no effort. Better yet, kids usually act as the guides, leading parents to take an interest in bugs of all kinds. Flying insects are easy to watch with no effort at all as they pass through backyards, meadows, playgrounds and picnic areas. A quick turn of a rock, a pull of dead, shaggy bark or the lifting of a rotten log reveals a flurry of activity as beetles, earwigs and centipedes scurry underground. A quick dip in a river current is sure to reveal stoneflies, mayflies, caddisflies and more. Kids love insects and other bugs because they are easy to find!

FUN TO WATCH

Bug behaviors are as diverse as the animals themselves and best of all, they occur in a space and scale to which small people can relate quite easily. Roly-polies curl into balls at the slightest touch; dragonflies are as colorful as a rainbow as they hunt above marshes and waterways; bees feed and gather busily as they hover from flower to flower. Simple observation of a diversity of bugs reveals an enormous display of colors, behaviors and designs, all capable of catching attention and entertaining a child's curiosity for hours, on sleepy summer afternoons.

EXCITING TO CATCH

Catching bugs is good for a child's mental health and exploratory nature. People should not catch mammals or birds, reptiles should be stalked with caution and knowledge and amphibians are fun to catch, but are not entirely common in the Rocky Mountains. Bugs, however, are exciting to catch and many fit comfortably in the palms of even the youngest hands.

SLIGHT DANGER

Except for allergic reactions, bugs in the Rocky Mountains pose little threat of danger. Nobody is going to lose a limb or be chased down in fright while searching for bugs. That said, accidents do happen. Disturbed bees and wasps can cause a fright and a sting, ticks can linger too long on a child's skin and kids can react strongly to seemingly slight incidences. Parents should be aware of where children are exploring and better yet, are encouraged to join in the outdoor adventures.

family field guide

Contents

How To Use This Book   **10**
Classification   **11**
Importance of Bugs   **12**
Bug-watching Tips   **13**
Insect Features   **14**
Insect Challenges   **15**
Symbols   **16**

Aquatic Bugs
Backswimmers   18
Caddisflies   20
Damselflies   22
Dragonflies   22
Mayflies   24
Mosquitoes   26
Scuds   28
Stoneflies   30
Water Boatmen   32
Water Striders   34
Whirligig Beetles   36

Ground Dwellers
Ants   38
Centipedes   40
Crickets   42
Daddy Longlegs   44
Earthworms   46
Earwigs   48
Millipedes   50
Roly-polies   52
Spiders   54

Plant Climbers
Gall Makers   56
Grasshoppers   58
Ladybugs   60
Slugs   62
Spittlebugs   64
Tent Caterpillars   66
Ticks   68

Flying Insects
Bees   70
Butterflies   72
 Brushfoots   74
 Gossamer-wings   76
 Swallowtails   78
 Whites and Sulphurs   80
Moths   82
Wasps   84

Appendices
Metamorphosis   86
Pollution Tolerance Index   88
What They Eat and Where   89
Award Winners   90
Butterfly Pictures   92
Moth Pictures   94

Glossary   **96**
Index   **98**
References   **99**

How To Use This Book

PURPOSE

This book is intended to enrich the outdoor explorations of children and families. Thirty of the most commonly observed and easy-to-identify bugs have been selected as an introduction to bug- life in the Rocky Mountains. These common species represent a broad enough diversity of behaviors and characteristics to gain an understanding of insects and other bugs in this region.

ORGANIZATION

The bugs in this book are organized according to the habitat in which they are most commonly observed. Within each of these habitat sections, the bugs are organized alphabetically. For example, water bugs are first, and are arranged alphabetically within this category. Next are soil dwellers, then plant feeders, then aerial fliers. Though bees and butterflies (especially caterpillars) are commonly observed feeding on plants, they are included with other fliers.

CLASSIFICATION

Though most readers, young and old alike, are not entirely interested in insect classification, the classification charts describe related animals and help to illustrate the incredible diversity within the world of insects and other crawly things!

SYMBOLS

As in all the books in this series, symbols are used to describe quickly and easily some of the essential information to understanding and identifying each bug. Look at the symbol at the top of each animal page, then refer back to the symbols page (p. 16-17) to understand its meaning.

PHOTOS AND ILLUSTRATIONS

The pictures provided on each page are designed to show unique and interesting elements of each animal's natural history. Some demonstrate life cycle, others may show specific behaviors, but each is used to demonstrate something remarkable and beautiful that text alone cannot capture.

APPENDICES

Pages at the back of the book are used to describe general information about insects and other bugs described within these pages.

family field guide

Classification

Identifying insects is no different than identifying mammals, birds or any other living thing. Insect identification, however, is difficult because there are so many of them. Scientists have identified over 1,000,000 different insect species worldwide. By comparison, 5,000 mammal species are known thoughout the world.

Insects, and all living things, are classified into categories based on their common features. Understanding how animals are classified provides a better understanding of insects in general. Following is a chart which shows how the insects and other bugs within this book are grouped and classified.

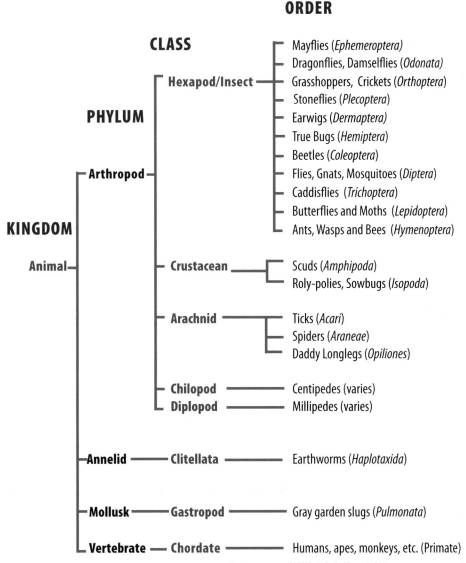

ORDER

CLASS

Hexapod/Insect
- Mayflies (*Ephemeroptera*)
- Dragonflies, Damselflies (*Odonata*)
- Grasshoppers, Crickets (*Orthoptera*)
- Stoneflies (*Plecoptera*)
- Earwigs (*Dermaptera*)
- True Bugs (*Hemiptera*)
- Beetles (*Coleoptera*)
- Flies, Gnats, Mosquitoes (*Diptera*)
- Caddisflies (*Trichoptera*)
- Butterflies and Moths (*Lepidoptera*)
- Ants, Wasps and Bees (*Hymenoptera*)

PHYLUM

Arthropod

Crustacean
- Scuds (*Amphipoda*)
- Roly-polies, Sowbugs (*Isopoda*)

Arachnid
- Ticks (*Acari*)
- Spiders (*Araneae*)
- Daddy Longlegs (*Opiliones*)

Chilopod — Centipedes (varies)
Diplopod — Millipedes (varies)

KINGDOM

Animal

Annelid — **Clitellata** — Earthworms (*Haplotaxida*)

Mollusk — **Gastropod** — Gray garden slugs (*Pulmonata*)

Vertebrate — **Chordate** — Humans, apes, monkeys, etc. (Primate)

family field guide

Importance of Bugs

WHY ARE BUGS IMPORTANT? Like most children, insects and other bugs perform a long list of chores. They pollinate plants, loosen soil, feed fish, birds, reptiles, amphibians and mammals and some even hunt each other so that their populations don't grow out of control. Some are considered pests at times, especially mosquitoes, wasps and grasshoppers that may destroy farmers' crops. However, in the big picture of life on this planet, bugs are equally as important, if not more important, as larger, prettier, cuddlier animals.

THE JOB CREW Part of the reason that insects do their chores so well is because there are so many of them. There are more unique species of insects in the world than any other group of animal. Each related group of bugs has a different set of chores to accomplish. For example, roly-polies loosen the soil and eat dead leaves, bees pollinate flowers, mayflies clean up the rivers, and wasps control insect populations so that they don't get out of control! Equally important to the diversity of species is the incredible number of individuals within each species. With so many individuals, the jobs are certain to get done well and on time! For comparison, there are 300,000,000 people in the United States, and there may be nearly that number of roly-polies within one square mile of soil on a single ranch! With so many roly-polies, the soil is certain to be plowed and the dead stuff is sure to be eaten. This abundance of insect life is vital to the existence of all ecosystems.

FOOD CHAIN All animals are important in the food chain, but bugs serve a variety of functions within the chain that are the foundation of healthy ecosystems. Most obviously, they are food for all types of animals (even for people in some cultures!). Less obviously, bees pollinate plants and without them we would not have apples, peaches, pumpkins or other vegetables. Many bugs also till the soil so that water and air can move easily through the soil into the roots of plants. This team of flying pollinators and underground tillers ensures that our earth is covered with plants to supply the world with food (and oxygen, too).

DECOMPOSERS In the same way that children need to clean up their rooms and put their dishes away after dinner, a team of insects, other bugs, bacteria and fungi are in charge of cleaning up the dead leaves and dead bodies of the earth. Much of the clean-up crew is so small that they are difficult to see, but roly-polies, earthworms and millipedes are easy-to-recognize decomposers. Scuds serve the same function in ponds, wetlands and lakes. Without these important bugs, our earth would pile up with dead stuff, suffocating the life out all of us...not to mention the earth would smell really bad, too!

family field guide

Bug-watching Tips

CAUTION!!! Be careful not to trample sensitive natural environments or high-use recreation areas while hunting for bugs and remember that collecting *any* type of animal is prohibited in national parks, national recreation areas, national monuments and state parks.

WATER BUGS Catching water bugs is one of the most sensory-engaging and hands-on sources of outdoor entertainment for youngsters and adults alike. First, fill a clear cup or jar with stream water which will act as a holding tank. Next, roll over a few rocks within a shallow part of a stream or riverbed and see what is attached to them. If no bugs are found, place a small net in a shallow stream current and roll over rocks upstream so that larvae might flow into the net. Study the contents of the net carefully, looking for any movement among the dirt and debris caught in the net. In stagnant water, simply swish the net back and forth among plant litter on the pond's edge. Any bugs that are caught can be placed in the holding tank for observation.

SOIL DWELLERS Finding insects and bugs beneath rocks and logs provides the most simple form of bug hunting. Simply roll over rocks or logs in any forest or grassland and look quickly before the earwigs, centipedes, millipedes, roly-polies, ants, earthworms and beetles scurry quickly below ground.

PLANT FEEDERS Finding caterpillars, ladybugs and other insects that hide among plants is as simple as looking carefully within the leaves of small shrubs, grasses or trees. To see the greatest diversity of activity, hold a large butterfly net beneath the leaves and branches of a small shrub or branch and shake the foliage firmly. You'll be surprised to see what is hiding among the leaves and branches as they fall into your net!

IN FLIGHT Catching butterflies and dragonflies in flight is a fun, but often difficult task as they commonly fly out of reach. For best results, use a large butterfly net and approach slowly in a quiet, stalking manner. Once within reach, angle the net downward over the top of the insect. This activity provides great entertainment for energetic children and for parents as well as they watch their kids exploring natural settings with great focus. Be sure to set parameters as children can easily twist an ankle or trip over debris hidden beneath grasses or on a forest floor.

OBSERVATION Once bugs are collected, use a camera, hand lens, magnifying glass or low-powered microscope to see small details. Take note of mouth parts, eyes, gills of aquatic larvae, feet and antennae. These details can send a youngster's imagination and sense of wonder to new heights!

Insect Features

All insects have the following features in common:

SIX LEGS

All insects have six legs which appear in many different shapes and sizes depending on the insect's lifestyle. Ladybugs, for example, have three sets of legs that are all quite short and are designed for climbing up skinny plants. Water striders have legs of varying sizes, each of which serves a different function. Regardless of size and shape, all insects have six legs; in contrast, *arachnids* have eight.

THREE BODY PARTS

Every insect has three body parts. The *head* is made up of eyes, antennae and mouth parts. Many insects are classified based on their mouth parts which are designed either for chewing or sucking their food. The middle section is called the *thorax* which provides support for the three pairs of jointed legs and for wings if they are present. The *abdomen* is the back end of the insect and contains organs for digesting food, excreting and for making babies.

ANTENNAE

All insects have two *antennae* which are important for sensing their surroundings. These delicate features act as the nose, fingers, ears and more. They are used to sense direction, motion, humidity, sound, smell and chemicals in the air. Antennae (plural for antenna) come in many different shapes and sizes depending on the insect's lifestyle. Some are long and skinny, others are feathery and some are short and wide.

EXOSKELETON

Insects have a hard, shell-like *exoskeleton,* or *cuticle,* on the outside of the body. This cuticle supports the insect's body and protects against injury. Muscles attach to the inside of the cuticle so the body can move while they are protected against small predators. As an immature insect grows, its cuticle splits open, a soft insect pushes out and the new, outer cuticle soon hardens. This shedding process is called *molting*.

family field guide

Insect Challenges

Many people enjoy watching insects, but have a difficult time understanding how they work. Following are some of the challenges that people face when learning about insects and ways this book addresses these challenges.

VOCABULARY

Scientists have created thousands of words to describe insect life which are not common to everyday language. These unfamiliar words make the initial task of studying insects similar to learning a foreign language. This book uses simple language when possible and provides an easy-to-use glossary for words specific to *entomology* (the study of insects).

METAMORPHOSIS

Insects grow from "childhood" to adulthood in a different way from mammals, birds, fish and other familiar animals. Young insects often look totally different from their adult form. For example, caterpillars and butterflies look nothing alike, but they are the same animal, one the immature "child," the other a mature adult. This unfamiliar growth pattern, called *metamorphosis*, is important when observing, identifying and understanding insects, but can be intimidating because of its uniqueness. This book gives clear reference to metamorphosis (see p. 86-87) and tells how each insect grows.

SIZE AND MOVEMENT

While some insects are easy to observe during certain parts of their life cycle, their size and movements make them difficult to understand entirely. For example, adult mosquitoes are everywhere and are easy to identify, but the immature *larvae* hide below the surface of water making them difficult to observe and to understand completely. This book explains in simple language some of the hard-to-see life history of common insects.

ABUNDANCE

There are more insect species in the world than there are people in many cities. This diversity is intimidating and makes some people want to give up before attempting to make sense of even the most common insects. This book describes the most common groups of insects without going into the daunting details of individual species. It also provides a classification comparison (p. 11) to help make sense of how insects and other bugs are related.

Symbols

Look at the symbols on each insect page, then read the explanations below to understand their meanings.

HABITAT Describes the habitat where the insect may live.

AQUATIC INSECTS

The *immature* stages of the bug develop in water. The adult is usually found near water, too.

SOIL DWELLERS

All stages of the bug's development are most commonly found on the ground among dead leaves, grasses, rocks and other plant matter.

PLANT CLIMBERS

All phases of the bug's development are most commonly found within leaves and branches of living plants.

FLYING INSECTS

The *immature* phases develop in trees or underground and adults are most commonly observed flying in parks, forests and meadows.

LIFE CYCLE Describes the insect's development from egg to adulthood.

NO METAMORPHOSIS
The animal is not an insect and does not develop through metamorphosis.

INCOMPLETE METAMORPHOSIS
The bug grows from an egg, the nymph molts several times then matures to an adult which is able to reproduce.

COMPLETE METAMORPHOSIS
The insect grows from an egg, molts several times as a *larva* and enters a non-feeding *pupal* phase before growing to an adult which is able to reproduce.

family field guide

FOOD Describes feeding habits during the immature and adult stages.

HERBIVORE
The bug eats only plants; leaves, sap or stems.

PREDATOR
The bug kills and eats other bugs.

SCAVENGER/DECOMPOSER
The bug eats dead and decaying matter including dead plants or animals.

POLLINATOR
The bug eats pollen or nectar from plants.

OMNIVORE
The bug eats other animals and plants.

LOOK Compares the appearance of the immature insect with the adult.

DIFFERENT
The immature looks very different from the adult.

SAME
The immature looks similar or identical to the adult.

TYPE Describes the animal's classification as an insect or other bug.

INSECT
This animal is an insect.

NON-INSECT
This animal is not an insect.

Backswimmers

HABITAT

LIFE CYCLE

TYPE

LOOK

FOOD

John Rushenberg

CLASSIFICATION

Kingdom Animal
Phylum Arthropod
Class Insect
Order *Hemiptera* (True Bugs)
Family *Notonectidae*
32 species in North America; 200 species worldwide.

IDENTIFICATION

Nymph Similar body shape and size as adults, but with a light colored body.
Adult Oval-shaped body, long hind legs with tiny "hairs," swim on their backs.

LIFE CYCLE

Incomplete metamorphosis
egg-nymph-adult

FOOD

Nymph Other water insects, tadpoles, small fish and other backswimmer nymphs.
Adult Same as nymphs.

HABITAT

Nymph Ponds, lakes and other slow-moving bodies of water.
Adult Same as nymphs.

WATER WASP As with all insects in the order *Hemiptera*, backswimmers have a needle-like mouth. While they are predators and eat other animals, they do not have two sets of jaws used for chewing. Instead they inject their needle-nose into the prey and suck out the insides like a milk shake. If handled carelessly, backswimmers are known to "sting" causing a pinch comparable to a bee sting. This biting characteristic is cause for other common names including "water bee" and "water wasp."

FLIPPERS Backswimmers' legs serve several different purposes. The front legs are used for catching and holding prey while the hind legs do most of the swimming. The hind legs are a bit wider than the other legs and are fringed with tiny hairs. These hairs create a wider swimming surface much like flippers which allow faster swimming. They are also much longer than the other legs so that they have a longer range of motion, again allowing a strong pull for fast swimming.

AIR SUPPLY Backswimmers must come to the water surface to breathe. They may be seen "resting" upside down, barely beneath the water surface, with their tail poking through to the air above. In this instance, the backswimmer is breathing and creating an air bubble which it stores on its belly. This air bubble provides enough oxygen to stay under water up to six hours before returning to the surface for more air.

family field guide

LOOK ALIKES

Backswimmers, water boatmen and whirligig beetles are commonly confused. Backswimmers are most easily distinguished by their simple characteristic of swimming on their back. After catching an insect from a pond, place it in a bowl filled with bit of water; if you can see its eyes, it is a water boatman and if you see its legs and belly, it is a backswimmer.

WINGS

Adult backswimmers have fully-developed wings and are very good fliers. They can easily fly from one pond to another until they find a clean pool with a good food supply. For this reason, they are not good indicators of water quality, as their presence may only be temporary before moving on to cleaner water.

NAME

Unlike most Latin names, the name *Notonecta* has the same meaning as the common name. *Noto* is Greek for "back," and *necta* is Greek for "swimming."

Garry Pfaffmann

Garry Pfaffmann

Top View Backswimmers reveal a top view of their body when removed from water.

Exoskeleton Like all arthropods, backswimmers leave their exoskeleton behind after each molt.

family field guide

Caddisflies

HABITAT

LIFE CYCLE

LOOK

TYPE

IMMATURE

ADULT

Garry Pfaffmann

CLASSIFICATION

Kingdom Animal
Phylum Arthropod
Class Insect
Order *Trichoptera* (Caddisflies)
190 species in Colorado; over 50,000 species worldwide.

IDENTIFICATION

Larva Soft-bodied, 6-legged worm; usually inside a casing made of pebbles, leaves, twigs or mud.
Adult At rest, wings are held tent-like over the back; long, thin antennae.

LIFE CYCLE

Complete metamorphosis
egg-larva-pupa-adult

FOOD

Larva Dead leaves, algae, smaller aquatic insect larvae.
Adult Do not eat solids, but may feed on nectar or other liquids.

HABITAT

Larva In cold, fast-moving water.
Adult In trees or in the air near open water.

NAME The Latin name *Trichoptera* refers to the hairy wings of the adults (*trich*-hair; *optera*-wings). Adult caddisflies look like delicate moths. The two are in fact closely related; both produce silk and are attracted to light. Moths, however, open their wings wide while resting; caddisflies hold their wings tent-like over their body and do not have a beak-like *proboscis*.

ARCHITECTS Caddisfly *larvae* live in water. They are commonly found in large rivers, small streams, ponds, lakes and marshes. They are most easily identified by the hard cases (pictured above) or silken *retreats* which they build around their soft, worm-like bodies. The designs of the cases or retreats vary by species, and may be built of rocks, leaves, stems, twigs or even mud. The soft bodied larva inside the retreat spins sticky silk which is used as a glue to attach materials from the river bottom, stream or pond. In this way, caddisfly larvae make their own shelter.

PUPA Unlike stoneflies, mayflies and true bugs, caddisflies undergo complete metamorphosis similar to butterflies. Once the larvae grow to maturity, they attach their retreats or cases to rocks or branches in the water, close off the opening and begin the transformation into adulthood. Once they mature, they chew through the opening of the case with sharp mouth parts and swim to the surface. Their mouthparts lose all chewing function once they emerge as adults.

family field guide

DIVERSITY

Caddisflies are the most diverse order of insects in which *all* of its members are aquatic. The most obvious differences between most species are the unique designs used in their retreats. Scientists, however, look carefully at at the differences between male and female reproductive organs to identify the exact species.

CLEAN WATER

Along with mayflies and stoneflies, caddisflies are important *indicators* of water quality. Different types of caddisfly larvae can live in varying amounts of pollution, so they are not perfect indicators of clean water. If, however, many different types of caddisfly larvae live in streambeds, the water is likely very clean (see page 88).

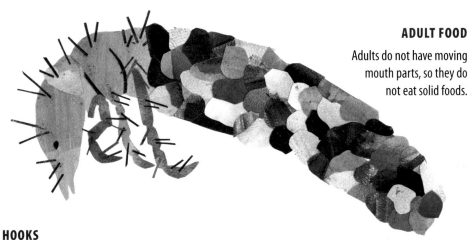

ADULT FOOD

Adults do not have moving mouth parts, so they do not eat solid foods.

HOOKS

Caddisfly larvae are worm-like, but are most easily identified by their shell-like casings. The wormy body inside has hooks at the tail end which hold on tightly to the casing so that it does not wash away. All six legs of the larvae are located near the front of the body so they can extend out of the casing as they walk along the rocks, dragging their protected body along behind them. When disturbed the larvae are able to pull their bodies into the casing for protection.

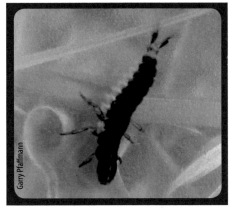

Hooks Hooks at the tail end of the worm-like caddisfly larva hold onto the silken *retreat*.

Adult Caddisfly adults hold their wings tent-like over their backs and are colored like many moths.

Dragonflies and Damselflies

HABITAT

LIFE CYCLE

LOOK

TYPE

FOOD

CLASSIFICATION

Kingdom Animal
Phylum Arthropod
Class Insect
Order *Odonata* (Dragonflies and Damselflies)
108 species in Colorado; over 5,000 Dragonfly and Damselfly species worldwide.

IDENTIFICATION

Nymph Short, fat bodies, large eyes, three gills on each side of the abdomen.
Adult Long, colorful body, four wings, big eyes.

LIFE CYCLE

Incomplete metamorphosis
egg-nymph-adult

FOOD

Nymph Aquatic larvae of other insects.
Adult Flying insects, especially mosquitoes, flies, bees and butterflies.

HABITAT

Nymph In cold, fast-moving water.
Adult Usually near marshes; sometimes over grassy meadows.

DRAGONFLIES AND DAMSELFLIES Dragonflies and damselflies are similar in shape, but dragonflies are thicker while damselflies are smaller and more delicate. Also, dragonflies spread their wings flat while at rest, while damselflies (*pictured above*) fold their wings over their tail. Dragonflies are more active, can fly farther, faster, higher and often mate in the air. Damselflies are thinner, remain nearer to the ground and usually mate on leaves or other surfaces.

POND FLIERS Adult dragonflies can fly as fast as some birds and are able to cover long distances in a short amount of time. Nonetheless, they are mostly found near ponds and marshes for two reasons. First, dragonfly nymphs grow under water, so newly hatched adults may have just emerged from the water where they are observed. Second, they eat other flying insects and often hunt where other adult insects are hatching. However, because they can feed on any type of flying insect, they may also be observed in meadows and other areas far from water.

PEST CONTROL Many people love dragonflies because of their colorful bodies, their beautiful flight, their large compound eyes and the intricate vein patterns in their wings. These carnivores also help control mosquito and fly populations, which can make a visit to a favorite lake, pond or marsh a bit more comfortable for we two-legged visitors.

family field guide

FLIGHT

The four wings of dragonflies and damselflies are not connected, so each can move independently from the others. This freedom of motion allows them to fly up, down, forward, backward or to hover in one place, making them remarkable acrobats of aquatic air space.

FOOD CHAIN

Dragonflies are fierce insect predators. Larvae are underwater carnivores while adults hunt the airways above the water. They are, however, common prey for birds so adults rarely live more than a month.

Damselfly

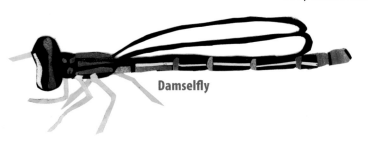

Dragonfly

ANCIENT INSECT

Fossils of dragonflies have been identified dating back as far as 200 million years. Back in these prehistoric years, a dragonfly's wingspan was over two feet from tip-to-tip. Dragonflies today have a wingspan of 3-6 inches, depending on the species.

EYES

Dragonflies have huge, *compound eyes*. Each of their two eyes is made up of many smaller eyes which work together to see. These large compound eyes allow a broad field of vision so they can see both predators and prey as they fly.

Nymph This final cast of a dragonfly nymph's outer skin remains attached to a cattail leaf as the adult breaks through the skin to hunt the airways.

Adult Adult dragonflies have a colorful *thorax*, beautifully patterned wings and huge compound eyes.

family field guide

Mayflies

Drew Shields

HABITAT

LIFE CYCLE

LOOK

TYPE

FOOD

CLASSIFICATION
Kingdom Animal
Phylum Arthropod
Class Insect
Order *Ephemeroptera* (Mayflies)
104 species in Colorado; over 2,500 species worldwide.

IDENTIFICATION
Nymph Delicate body, 2 or 3 tails, one claw on each leg, gills along both sides of the abdomen.
Adult Wings held upward while resting, two long tails, thin body is usually curved upward while at rest.

LIFE CYCLE
Incomplete metamorphosis
egg-nymph-subadult-adult

FOOD
Nymph Mostly algae or dead and decaying plant material.
Adult Does not feed.

HABITAT
Nymph In cold, fast-moving water; some live in standing water.
Adult In trees or in the air near water.

NAME *Ephemeral* means short-lived. The Latin name *Ephemeroptera* refers to the mayfly's short lifespan. While nymphs might live up to a full year underwater, adults live only a few hours up to a day before they die or are eaten by fish, birds or larger insects. Adult mayflies have such a short life that they do not have any mouth parts at all! Obviously they do not eat a single meal during their few short hours of life. Because of their short lifespan, they are called "One Day Flies" in several languages.

UNIQUE MOLT The word *imago* is a fancy word meaning "adult." Mayflies are unique in their life cycle because they have a subadult phase after they hatch from the water and before they are reproducing adults. They are the only insect that *molts* their wings as an adult. Once a mayfly nymph swims to a rock or blade of grass, it breaks through its *cuticle* and an adult mayfly is born. However, this adult, called a *subimago*, is not yet able to reproduce. The subimago waits on a rock or log while its body dries and its wings harden, then it flies off to the protection of a tree. Once at the tree, it molts out of its skin *again*, and a true adult is born. Scientists continue to debate why mayfly adults have this intermediate molting which takes place between the nymph and true adult phase.

family field guide

SWARMS

Nymphs of many water species hatch under specific temperatures, cloud cover and seasonal conditions. For this reason, thousands of individuals of specific species will hatch all at the same time. When a *hatch* occurs, huge swarms of mayflies, or other water insects, gather above the water. Within these swarms, males and females are looking to mate. Mayflies often fly directly up and down, as if they are bouncing in the air, as they seek out their mates.

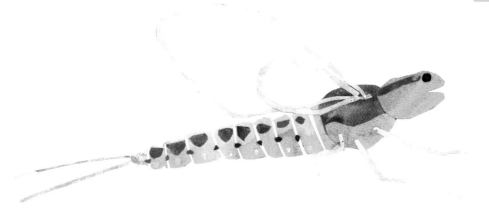

WATER QUALITY

Mayfly larvae cannot live in polluted waters. A healthy population of mayfly nymphs in a river, stream or lake indicates that the water is very clean (see page 88).

TAME ADULT

More than any other insect, except mosquitoes, mayflies are likely to land on the shoulder or hat brim of a passing hiker. This tame demeanor invites an easy, close-up look at the curved body and vertical wing display of this delicate and beautiful insect.

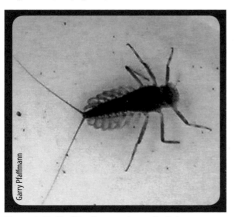

Nymph Tails Mayfly nymphs and adults can have two tails (above) or three (right).

Nymph Claws Mayfly nymphs have a single claw on each foot, while stoneflies have two claws.

family field guide

Mosquitoes

HABITAT

LIFE CYCLE

LOOK

TYPE

FEMALE

MALE

USDA

CLASSIFICATION

Kingdom Animal
Phylum Arthropod
Class Insect
Order *Diptera* (mosquitoes, flies, gnats)
Family *Culicidae* (mosquitoes)
44 species in Colorado; over 3,000 species worldwide.

IDENTIFICATION

Larva Worm the size of a grain of rice, with a breathing tube pointed upward; called "wrigglers."
Pupa Active, wiggly-worm; large head and worm-like body; called "tumblers."
Adult Long delicate legs, obvious beak or *proboscis*, transparent wings.

LIFE CYCLE

Complete metamorphosis
egg-larva-pupa-adult

FOOD

Larva Algae and bacteria filtered from water.
Adult Males feed on nectar; females feed on nectar and blood from animals.

HABITAT

Larva and Pupa Near the surface of stagnant or slow-moving water.
Adult In the air, especially near water.

WATER Because mosquito eggs are laid in water and the first stages of their life cycle occur in water, adult mosquitoes are most abundant in wet, marshy areas. Larvae and pupae grow best in stagnant water, but may be found on the edges of large, slow-moving rivers as well. Flooded pastures, meadows wet with melted snow, pooled rain gutters and boggy wetlands are all excellent habitat for mosquito development.

BUG BITES Female mosquitoes suck blood from animals because they need the protein to produce eggs. As they poke their "beaks" into the skin, they inject saliva which contains chemicals that allow them to digest the blood. One of these chemicals stops blood from clotting (called an *anticoagulant*) so that she can drink it easily. When these anticoagulants enter a person's body, the immune system sends a team of cells called *histamines* to attack the invading chemicals. The itchy swollen bump that forms from a mosquito bite is the result of the reaction between your body's histamines and the mosquito's saliva.

FOOD CHAIN Humans seem to have met their match when it comes to controlling mosquito bites. Hundreds of formulas have been developed to prevent these pesky bites, but none are 100% effective. Mosquitoes are perhaps the best representative in the animal kingdom to remind us, that we are part of, and not always at the top of, the food chain.

family field guide

DISEASE CARRIER

Some people argue that the mosquito is the most dangerous animal in the world. Female mosquitoes suck blood from a variety of animals, sometimes collecting disease-carrying germs in the process. The diseases are then passed on to the next animal or person they bite. Mosquitoes are carriers of some of the most dangerous diseases in the world including malaria, yellow fever and dengue fever, none of which occur in the United States. In the U.S., however, some are carriers of West Nile virus, a virus that first appeared in the U.S. in 1999. Birds carry the West Nile virus, then mosquitoes which feed on their blood collect the virus. As they bite horses, people, chipmunks and other animals, the virus spreads.

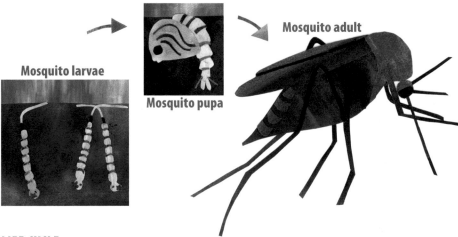

Mosquito larvae

Mosquito pupa

Mosquito adult

LIFE CYCLE

Mosquito eggs are usually laid in shallow stagnant water. The *larvae* hatch and hang upside down with their tail poking up to the surface of the water. They breathe through their tail which receives oxygen from the air above the water. After molting three times, they enter their *pupal* stage in which they are active wiggly-worms for several days. As with all insects, the *pupae* do not eat. After the mosquito grows to adulthood inside this cuticle, it wiggles to the surface of the water and the adult climbs onto a rock or stick to dry before flying away. The female is able to bite within two days after molting to adulthood.

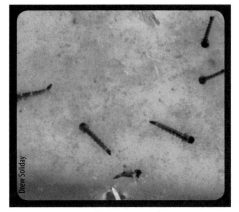

Larva Mosquito larvae, called "wrigglers" float near the surface of shallow water.

Habitat Mosquitoes lay eggs in ponds, wetlands and other slow-moving or stagnant water sources.

Scuds

HABITAT

LIFE CYCLE

LOOK

TYPE

FOOD

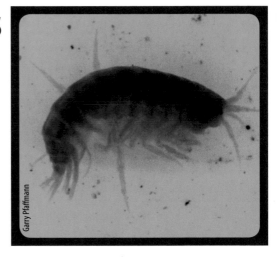

Garry Pfaffmann

CLASSIFICATION

Kingdom Animal
Phylum Arthropod
Class Crustacean (Crabs, Lobsters, Shrimp)
Order Amphipod (Scuds)
About 6 species in Colorado; about 800 freshwater species worldwide.

IDENTIFICATION

Young and Adult Small, shrimp-looking animal the size of a child's pinky fingernail; transparent body; swim on their sides.

LIFE CYCLE

Incomplete metamorphosis
Scuds are not insects, but molt as they grow.

FOOD

Young and Adult Mostly dead plant and animal matter.

HABITAT

Young and Adult Along the edge and bottom of ponds and slow-moving water.

NOT AN INSECT Scuds are *crustaceans*, not insects; they are more closely related to shrimp, crayfish and lobster than to mayflies, stoneflies or caddisflies.

LIFE CYCLE Crustaceans, unlike insects, do not change form during their lifetime; like humans, young scuds look similar to adults. Males and females mate in spring and early summer. They are easily observed swimming together before mating occurs. Pregnant females are easy to identify by a dark-colored patch on their bodies. This dark patch is where females carry eggs and the developing babies. The babies are born after about three weeks inside the mother, who usually dies following their birth. The young are full grown by October, hide out under rocks through winter, then mate the following spring.

DECOMPOSER Scuds live in high mountain ponds and lakes and in many streams and rivers. They eat dead animal and plant matter off the muddy bottoms. Animals that eat dead plant and animal matter are called *decomposers* and play the very important role of cleaning up the dead litter from ecosystems. A healthy scud population is important in slow moving water, because they help to clean the dead stuff that drops to the bottom of the water. Dead stuff flows downstream in rivers, but in ponds and marshes, a cleaning crew is needed to eat all of the dead matter that cannot float away.

family field guide

FISH FOOD

Scuds are a favorite meal for fish, so they rarely grow to maturity in fish-filled ponds. In water where fish are not present, scuds may grow to the size of an adult's pinky fingernail.

NOCTURNAL

Scuds are most active at night. They do not like light and spend most of the daylight hours hiding beneath rocks, logs, grasses or mud.

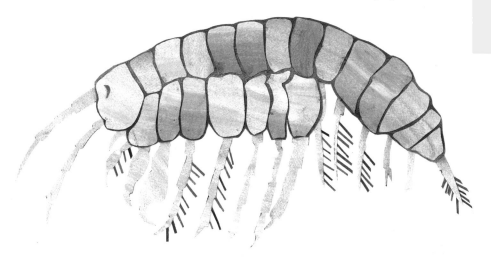

WATER QUALITY

Scuds can tolerate small amounts of pollution. Their presence tells scientists that ponds and lakes are not severely polluted, but they do not indicate clean water as much as the presence of stoneflies and mayflies (see page 88).

BOTTOM DWELLER

Scuds live among the muddy pond bottom for several reasons. First, most of the food they eat has died and sunk to the bottom of the pond or lake. Second, they can easily bury themselves in the mud when predators approach.

Garry Pfaffmann

Garry Pfaffmann

Mating Scuds are often observed in mating position as they scurry through shallow water.

Motion Scuds coil and recoil as they use their legs and body-motion to move.

family field guide

Stoneflies

HABITAT

LIFE CYCLE

LOOK

TYPE

IMMATURE

ADULT

Boris Kondratieff, Colorado State University

CLASSIFICATION

Kingdom Animal
Phylum Arthropod
Class Insect
Order *Plecoptera* (Stoneflies)
87 species in Colorado; over 2,000 species worldwide.

IDENTIFICATION

Nymph Two tails, very long antennae, two claws on each foot.
Adult At rest, wings overlap each other and rest flat down the back, extending beyond the end of the body.

LIFE CYCLE

Incomplete metamorphosis
egg-nymph-adult

FOOD

Nymph Larvae of other small insects, leaves and algae.
Adult Some species do not eat, others eat algae or lichen near water.

HABITAT

Nymph In cold, fast-moving water.
Adult On the ground or in trees near water.

NAME The name "stonefly" may refer to the stones or rocks where these nymphs live. Stoneflies lay eggs on the water surface, then the eggs sink to the bottom of the river. The eggs hatch underwater and nymphs live there for months or even years, depending on the species. While under water, the nymphs hide beneath rocks. The Latin name *Plecoptera* refers to the wings which fold on top of each other over their back while resting (*pleco*-folded; *ptera*-wing).

CLEAN WATER Scientists study the insects and other bugs that live in water as an *indicator* of any pollution that may be in the rivers, lakes or streams. Because stoneflies can only survive in clean water, scientists know that a large population of stonefly nymphs indicates clean water (see page 88).

ADULTHOOD After growing underwater for months or years, mature stonefly nymphs rise to the water surface. They crawl to a rock, bush or branch where they push their new wings out of the *cuticle*. The adults look similar to the nymphs, but for a newly added set of wings which extend beyond the tail. The adults fly clumsily to the cover of trees where they mate very quickly. Females then fly back over the water (some species dive into the water) where the eggs are laid. Adults are clumsy fliers and often make a mad splashing which attracts hungry fish.

family field guide

OXYGEN

Even though they don't have lungs, stonefly nymphs need a lot of oxygen. Fast-moving water usually has lots of oxygen, as does water that tumbles and churns over rocks. Therefore, stonefly nymphs usually live in fast-moving streams or rivers with a rocky bottom.

BIG NYMPH

Stonefly nymphs are among the largest insects found under water. They are often the size of a third grader's pinky. Because of their size, they are quite a meal for a small trout or a dipper (a bird that eats aquatic insects).

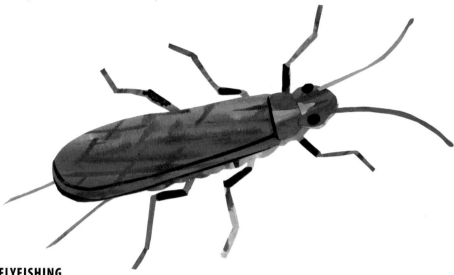

FLYFISHING

Because insects are a major food source for fish, fly fishermen and women use their knowledge of insects to trick the fish into biting their hooks. Though insect nymphs hide beneath rocks most of the time, insects frequently get caught in river currents or rise to the surface to hatch. In response, fish are constantly looking to eat these free-floating insects. People trying to catch fish make lures that look like specific types of insects at certain stages of development in their effort to trick the fish into biting their hooks. Stoneflies are one of the most important insects to fish and to the fishermen trying to catch them.

Adult Stonefly wings fold neatly over the back as the adult rests on trees near the water.

Flies Fly fishermen create elaborate designs to look like stonefly nymphs (left) and adults (right).

Water Boatmen

HABITAT   **LIFE CYCLE**

LOOK   **TYPE**   **FOOD**

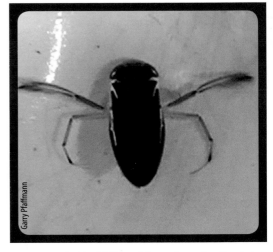
Garry Pfaffmann

CLASSIFICATION

Kingdom Animal
Phylum Arthropod
Class Insect
Order *Hemiptera* (true bugs)
Family *Corixidae* (water boatmen)
27 species in Colorado; 500 species worldwide.

IDENTIFICATION

Nymph Similar to adult, only smaller.
Adult Oval-shaped body, rounded head, very long hind legs extend forward.

LIFE CYCLE

Incomplete metamorphosis
egg-nymph-adult

FOOD

Nymph and Adult Suck the juices out of living plants; a few species feed on insect larvae in water.

HABITAT

Nymph and Adult In shallow lakes and ponds; sometimes they hide at the bottom, but they must come to the surface for air.

UNUSUAL BUG All "bugs" from the order *Hemiptera* have a needle-like mouth and are unable to chew. Instead, they poke their needle-nose into their food, inject their saliva which turns the insides of their prey to liquid, then they suck out the liquified food. Water boatmen have this same feeding style, but they are unique in that most species eat mostly plants! Some species can be *scavengers* feeding on the insides of other animals, but generally, boatmen rely mostly on plant juices for food.

FRINGED OARS The hind legs have a very long range of motion, extending forward beyond the head and pulling back towards the tail end. These long legs and large motion are designed for pulling, like the oars of a boat. These natural oars are fringed with hairs, allowing them to pull more water with each movement, also creating more power for faster swimming.

BREATHING Like all animals, water boatmen breathe oxygen, but they are not equipped with gills like stonefly and mayfly nymphs. Instead, they swim to the surface every few minutes to capture a bubble of air which they take with them back to the bottom of the pond. This air bubble acts like an oxygen tank from which they can breathe while feeding on plants at the lake bottom. When they run out of air, they swim to the surface for another bubble, and return again to feed on the bottom.

family field guide

FLIGHT

Water boatmen eggs are attached to plant stems within the water. When a nymph hatches, it immediately swims to the surface to catch a breath of air, then swims to the pond bottom for feeding. After molting several times it matures to an adult and forms wings. The adult immediately leaves the water on a "mating flight," then returns to the water where it continues to feed. Though it does not often use its wings for flight, it can fly to cleaner water sources if needed.

BOATMAN OR BACKSWIMMER?

Water boatmen are sometimes confused with backswimmers. Both have similar looking eyes and long hind legs which extend towards the head and are found in very similar habitats, among grasses in shallow ponds. However, water boatmen swim face-down while backswimmers swim on their backs!

INDICATOR

Water boatmen can live in a moderate amount of pollution and can fly between several water sources, so their presence in a pond does not necessarily indicate clean water (see page 88).

Adult Water Boatmen are the size of a watermelon seed with long hind legs for swimming.

Habitat Water boatmen swim in shallow water, and are easily observed diving along pond edges.

family field guide

Water Striders

HABITAT

LIFE CYCLE

LOOK

TYPE

FOOD

CLASSIFICATION

Kingdom Animal
Phylum Arthropod
Class Insect
Order *Hemiptera* (true bugs)
Family *Gerridae* (water striders)
12 species in Colorado; over 500 species worldwide.

IDENTIFICATION

Nymph Similar to the adult.
Adult Short front legs, long middle and hind legs, skinny body.

LIFE CYCLE

Incomplete metamorphosis
egg-nymph-adult

FOOD

Nymph and Adult Small live or dead insects mostly from the water surface; may dive for food.

HABITAT

Nymph and Adult On the surface of seasonal or permanent lakes and ponds; mostly in slow-moving or stagnant water.

FOOD Water striders eat other aquatic bugs. They may dive to the bottom to catch immature insects, but usually catch them as they rise to the surface. Like all True Bugs (order *Hemiptera)*, water striders have sucking mouth parts. Their mouth is shaped like a needle which they inject into the prey to suck out the liquid food. Water striders do not chew their food like you and me, instead, they suck the insides like a milkshake.

DIRTY WATER Water striders can live in polluted water. Because they do not live under the water, they are not as affected by pollution as insects which live beneath the water surface. Simply because water striders are living in a pond, does not mean that the water is clean (see page 88)!

WALKING ON WATER A water strider's ability to walk on water is quite unique among animals because they do not use friction as a means of moving across the water's slippery surface. Their legs and underbelly are covered with fine hairs. These hairs and the angle at which their legs hit the water help them to float without breaking the surface. While "walking," they use their middle legs to "row" in the same way a boatman uses oars to paddle a boat forward or backward. Their hind legs are used for steering, in the same way that a rudder steers a boat from the back side. Their shorter front legs are used for catching prey.

family field guide

VIBRATIONS

Water striders feel vibrations in the water and use them to hunt for prey or to hide from predators. Their feet, which ride on top of the water, can feel such tiny movements as a mosquito larva wriggling at the water surface. Small vibrations indicate that a meal is approaching. Large vibrations, such as that of an approaching fish, signal that they should skip quickly into hiding. During mating season they make ripples on the water to attract mates!

NAMES

Water striders have many different common names, all of which refer to their ability to walk on water. Some of the most commonly used names include Pond Skater, Pond Skipper, Water Skipper, Water Skimmer, Jesus Bug and more.

HIBERNATION

Water striders sometimes live in small pools which dry up by mid-summer. Because most do not fly, water striders are unable to move easily from pool to pool. Instead, they burrow into the mud where they hibernate until the pool fills again the following season. Water striders that survive through the summer and fall may hide inside a plant stem or between a mat of leaves where they hibernate until warm temperatures return.

Garry Pfaffmann

Shadow The shadows created by water striders are often noticed before the insects themselves.

Garry Pfaffmann

Mating Careful observation often reveals two striders together in mating position.

Whirligig Beetles

HABITAT

LIFE CYCLE

LOOK

TYPE

FOOD

Garry Pfaffmann

CLASSIFICATION
Kingdom Animal
Phylum Arthropod
Class Insect
Order *Coleoptera* (beetles)
Family *Gyrinidae* (whirligig beetles)
At least 8 species in Colorado; 700 species worldwide.

IDENTIFICATION
Larva Slender worm with many fringed strands dangling from its back half.
Adult Oval-shaped body, size of a watermelon seed, long front legs, short flattened middle and hind legs, shiny shell.

LIFE CYCLE
Complete metamorphosis
egg-larva-pupa-adult

FOOD
Larva Smaller aquatic insect larvae.
Adult Insects on the water surface; may dive for food, but must return to the surface for air.

HABITAT
Larva Hide at the bottom of lakes, ponds and slow-moving streams.
Adult Swim on the surface of lakes, ponds and slow-moving streams.

FLOATING BEETLE Whirligig beetles are usually observed swimming on the surface of lakes, ponds or slow-moving water. This is the only *beetle* that is able to float in water. Whirligigs often gather in large groups, called *rafts*, but they may be found individually as well. This rafting behavior is most commonly observed in mornings when temperatures are cool. As cold-blooded animals, these beetles need to warm their bodies before the day's activities can begin. The beetles gather together to share body heat in sunny places then, once warmed, individuals of most species disperse throughout the day. Some species raft together all day.

EYES Because they float on the water surface, whirligig beetles must watch for predators from above (mostly birds) and from below (mostly fish, but also large insect larvae). They have specialized eyes that are divided so they can see clearly both above and below water. If they see a predator in the air, they can dive to safety; if they see a predator below, they can fly to safety.

CHEMICAL DEFENSE When disturbed or threatened, whirligigs release a foul smelling chemical which is distasteful to fish. Some say the chemical smells sweet like apples, so they are sometimes called "apple bugs." This chemical, called *gyrinidal* is also the basis of their scientific name *Gyrinidae*.

family field guide

NAME

The common name "whirligig" comes from this beetle's behavior of spinning around and around in circles while swimming.

OXYGEN

When diving, adults create an air bubble and store it under their front legs. Under water, they use this air bubble as a breathing supply like a scuba diver's oxygen tank.

POLLUTION TOLERANT

Adult whirligigs can fly to other water sources. They may lirk in polluted water for a short time, then fly to better habitat. Therefore, their presence does not necessarily indicate clean water (see page 88).

LEGS

The two sets of hind legs on adult whirligigs are short and flattened. They are used like oars for paddling. The longer front legs are used for catching and holding onto prey. Adults feed mostly on insects that have fallen into the water from above, including those that are laying eggs on the water surface. When they see a mad splashing on the water, they quickly swim over to investigate, capture and carry their prey below water for feeding. In comparison, whirligig larvae swim below water and feed entirely on soft worms and other immature insect life within the water.

Habitat Whirligigs swim in shallow water, often hiding among cattails and other pond plants.

Whirling These beetles rarely stop moving as they whirl in circles on the surface of water.

Ants

Drew Soliday

HABITAT	LIFE CYCLE	LOOK

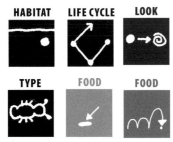

TYPE	FOOD	FOOD

CLASSIFICATION

Kingdom Animal
Phylum Arthropod
Class Insect
Order *Hymenoptera* (ants, wasps, bees)
Family *Formicidae* (ants)
At least 163 species in Colorado; over 8,800 species worldwide.

IDENTIFICATION

Larvae White, rice-sized grubs; only found within the nest.
Adult Three obvious body parts; worker ants (all females) are wingless; queen and reproductive males have wings.

LIFE CYCLE

Complete metamorphosis
egg-larva-pupa-adult

FOOD

Varies among species; may include dead insects, live insects, seeds, sweet foods, or greasy foods.

HABITAT

Varies among species; may be found in forests, grasslands, sidewalks or beneath rocks or dead logs.

TREES, MEADOWS AND SIDEWALKS Carpenter ants live in forests. As their name suggests, they dig tunnels and nests in rotted wood. Though they are larger in size than all other ants in Colorado, they are unable to bite through human skin. Harvester ants live in grasslands. They build mounds of pebbles and dirt above their nest sites and "harvest" all grasses from the surrounding area as they collect seeds for food. Red harvester ants bite, causing a stinging pinch that most people recognize. Pavement ants burrow between cracks in sidewalks, pushing dirt above ground leaving round dirt piles around their nesting sites.

CYCLE OF A COLONY An ant colony starts with a *queen* ant, a female that is able to reproduce. She starts her life with wings, mates with a winged male, flies to a nesting site and begins laying eggs. She immediately loses her wings. In the beginning, she gathers food, feeds the larvae and maintains the nest. Once the larvae develop to adulthood, these adults become the *workers* which collect food and take care of the nest. The queen is now responsible only for reproduction. She may live up to 15 years by which time several million ants may live in her colony. When the queen dies, the colony collapses.

family field guide

WINTER

The body heat created by ants within a colony is enough to keep a colony warm through the freezing winter months. Though they remain living, the colony becomes dormant and all egg-laying and feeding stops during winter.

Worker ants have many jobs. They maintain tunnels within the nest, collect food, fend off intruders and tend the larvae. Worker ants move the larvae to deeper parts of the nest at night to keep them warm, then move them close to the surface in the day to absorb the warmth of daytime temperatures.

LIFESPAN

While queen ants can live longer than 10 years, most workers live only 45-60 days.

COMMUNICATION

Ants must work together to ensure that food is collected, larvae are cared for and tunnels are maintained. To accomplish these tasks, they must communicate. Carpenter ants drum their heads on the ground to communicate through sound. Some ants communicate by touching with their antennae. The most important type of communication is through smell. Ants leave trails of chemicals called *pheromones* along feeding paths so that other ants can follow the stinky trail to food sources and bring food back to the colony.

Females Fertile male and female ants have wings and are much larger than worker ants.

Nest Worker ants care for eggs and larvae until they develop to adulthood.

family field guide

Centipedes

HABITAT

LIFE CYCLE

LOOK

TYPE

FOOD

Garry Pfaffmann

CLASSIFICATION
Kingdom Animal
Phylum Arthropod
Class *Chilopoda* (Centipedes)
About 25 species in Colorado; over 3,000 species worldwide.

IDENTIFICATION
Young and Adult Long, flattened body with one pair of legs per body segment.

LIFE CYCLE
Incomplete metamorphosis
Centipedes are not insects, but they molt.

FOOD
Young and Adult Small insects, spiders and worms; may eat smaller centipedes.

HABITAT
Young and Adult Dark, moist areas, especially beneath rocks, leaves and logs.

CARNIVORES All centipedes, no matter their size or species, are carnivores. They have sharp jaws that are attached to poison glands which stun and capture prey. They feed on other small animals living within the soil. Young earthworms are common prey as are smaller centipedes and millipedes. Most centipedes are too small to bite through human skin, but larger species may cause a "sting" similar in feeling to that of a bee.

WHAT'S THE DIFFERENCE? Identification of centipedes and millipedes is commonly confused. Quite simply, centipedes have one pair of legs per body segment while millipedes have two pairs of legs per segment. Also, centipedes usually have flatter bodies, while millipedes usually have rounded bodies, more like a shelled worm.

SOIL DWELLERS Centipedes are nighttime hunters that remain hidden beneath rocks, leaves and logs throughout the day. Their bodies dry out quickly when exposed to direct sunlight and dry conditions, so they typically hide out in shady, humid conditions. They prefer to remain hidden in or near the soil to lurk among their prey.

family field guide

HOW MANY LEGS?

While the name centipede refers to the number 100 (as in the word *century*), the number of legs varies greatly between species and age. As with all arthropods, these animals' bodies are segmented. The number of segments varies from 15 to 177 depending on the species, so the number of legs ranges from 30 to 354.

WORLD'S LARGEST

Centipedes in the Rocky Mountains usually range from 1-3 inches in length. The Giant Desert Centipede is located at lower elevations within Colorado and may grow to 6 inches in length. The largest known centipede in the world occurs in the Amazon rainforest and measures longer than 12 inches.

PESTS

Centipedes are commonly observed in houses and can survive indoors if they find a dark, moist environment. Because they eat other insects, these "pests" actually serve as pest control, but most homeowners prefer them to remain outdoors.

FAST-MOVING

Unlike roly-polies and millipedes, centipedes move very fast. After rolling a rock over, most observers get only a quick look at centipedes before they scurry into hiding.

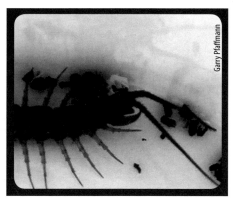

Legs and Claws A sharp set of claws near the head and mouth is used for catching prey. Antennae are used for feeling around their dark world.

Tunnels Centipedes use tiny tunnels to move through the soil. Notice the 3 legs sticking out from this hideout.

family field guide

Crickets

HABITAT

LIFE CYCLE

LOOK

TYPE

FOOD

FOOD

John Rusk...

CLASSIFICATION

Kingdom Animal
Phylum Arthropod
Class Insect
Order *Orthoptera* (crickets, grasshoppers)
Family *Gryllidae*
10 cricket and tree cricket species in Colorado;
900 species worldwide.

IDENTIFICATION

Young and Adult Brown to black in color,
antennae as long as the body, long back legs
for jumping.

LIFE CYCLE

Incomplete metamorphosis
Egg-nymph-adult

FOOD

Young and Adult Eat almost anything;
mostly plant matter, some smaller insects or
dead insects, dried and rotting plant matter;
may eat cloth in houses.

HABITAT

Young and Adult Dark, moist areas,
especially beneath rocks, leaves and logs or
in thick grasses.

CHIRPING Crickets are best known for their chirping sound which can be heard on warm evenings in summer. Only male crickets make the chirping sound which is mainly used to attract females. Different species have unique pitches so that females can respond to the calls of their own species. The sound is created by rubbing their wings together. The back side of each wing is hard and, when rubbed against a ridged vein on the other wing, a chirping sound is created. The wing rubbing action is similar to running a finger across the teeth of a comb, which also creates a high-pitched sound.

THERMOMETERS Because they are *cold-blooded* animals, the pace of a cricket's chirping is directly linked to temperature. The warmer the temperature, the less time between chirps. Dr. Amos E. Dolbear (one of the founders of the modern telephone) determined that cricket chirps are so closely related to air temperature, that they can be used to determine outside air temperature. His equation, called Dolbear's Law, is as follows: Temperature=50 + (N-40)/4 where N equals the number of chirps in one minute. Parents can help with this math problem!

PEST Crickets often find their way inside houses. Fortunately, their eggs cannot reproduce in a dry household environment, so those that accidentally wander in cannot lead to an *infestation* problem.

family field guide

MALES AND FEMALES

Both males and females have two sharp tails that extend at angles from the back side (called *cerci*), but only the female has the third "tail" which extends down the middle. This long tube is called an *ovipositor* and is used to lay eggs. The eggs are produced inside the body, then the long tube is poked into the soil and the eggs are dropped just beneath the surface.

DIFFERENCES

Though they are closely related, there are several important differences between crickets and grasshoppers. First, crickets have long antennae and the females have a long *ovipositor* (tail), while those of grasshoppers are short. Though adults of both crickets and grasshoppers have wings, crickets do not fly; most grasshopper species fly following their mighty leaps into the air.

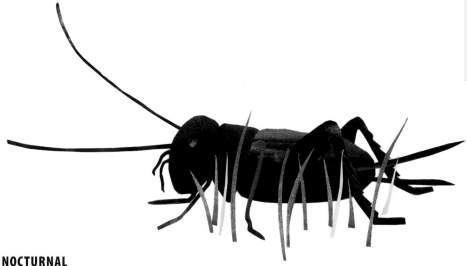

NOCTURNAL

Most crickets are *nocturnal*, becoming most active at night. For this reason, their chirps are more commonly heard on summer nights than during daylight hours.

EARS

A cricket's ears are located on its legs! A small hole on each front leg has an eardrum so they can hear the chirps of other crickets.

Pest Crickets are most commonly observed in houses along the edges of cabinets or baseboards.

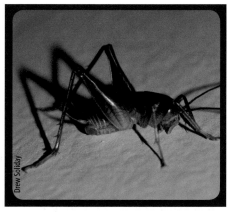

Tails Females appear to have three tails, while males (above) have only two.

Daddy Longlegs
(Harvestmen)

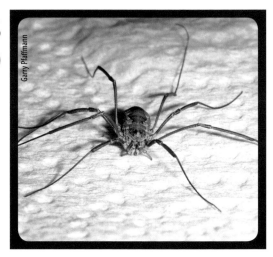

Garry Pfaffmann

HABITAT

LIFE CYCLE

LOOK

TYPE

FOOD

CLASSIFICATION
Kingdom Animal
Phylum Arthropod
Class Arachnid
Order *Opiliones* (Harvestmen)
Over 100 species in North America; about 3,500 species worldwide.

IDENTIFICATION
Young and Adult Single body part, eight very long legs, no web.

LIFE CYCLE
Incomplete metamorphosis
Though not an insect, they molt.

FOOD
Young and Adult Mostly decaying plant matter, but also a wide variety of bugs including aphids, mites, earthworms, slugs and caterpillars when possible.

HABITAT
Young and Adult Habitats vary by species, but generally they prefer dark, dry spaces beneath leaf cover, tree bark and among wood piles.

NON-SPIDER The name Daddy Longlegs most commonly refers to Harvestmen which are *arachnids*, but not spiders. Like all arachnids, they have four pairs of legs, but unlike spiders, they do not spin webs, do not produce venom and have only one pair of eyes compared with the three or four pairs for a spider.

POISONOUS MYTH A common urban myth suggests that Daddy Longlegs are the most poisonous of all spiders, but that their fangs cannot break human skin. First, if referring to the Harvestmen, they do not produce venom at all, so this is obviously a myth. Second, if referring to a Cellar Spider (*see page 55*), there have never been reports of any person being injured by this "daddy longlegs spider" and there is no scientific evidence that their venom is more toxic than an average spider toxin.

PROTECTION Daddy Longlegs are common prey for birds and spiders. Like all animals, Daddy Longlegs have several strategies for protection. If approached by danger, they release a foul smelling chemical to scare off potential predators. If that doesn't work, their legs pull off very easily, much like a lizards' tails, only their legs do not grow back. Loss of the second legs is especially dangerous because these legs have thousands of sensory nerves for feeling, smelling, tasting and understanding their surroundings.

family field guide

HARVEST SEASON

The name Harvestman most likely originated from the fact that these arachnids are most common in late summer and fall when farmers harvest their crops. Populations do seem to be highest during this time of year.

MALES AND FEMALES

Male Harvestmen have smaller bodies and longer legs while females have larger bodies and shorter legs.

MOLT

Like all arthropods, Daddy Longlegs molt as they grow. Watching them pull their long legs out of their old *cuticle* is quite a treat. Their molt occurs every ten days or so.

Legs The long skinny legs are the obvious reason for the common name Daddy Longlegs.

Non-spider Though it has four pairs of legs, the single body part and two eyes are not spider-like.

Earthworms

Garry Pfaffmann

CLASSIFICATION

Kingdom Animal
Phylum Annelid (segmented worms)
Class *Clitellata*
Order *Haplotaxida* (worms and leeches)
Family *Lumbricidae* (earthworms)
About 5 species in Colorado; over 2,700 species worldwide.

IDENTIFICATION

Young and Adult Soft, thin, segmented body.

LIFE CYCLE

No metamorphosis
Earthworms aren't insects and don't molt.

FOOD

Young and Adult Dead leaves, dried roots, small stones.

HABITAT

Young and Adult Within the top three inches of soil; burrow deeper during winter months.

SOIL BUILDER The famous naturalist Charles Darwin wrote, "It may be doubted whether there are many other creatures (besides the earthworm) which have played so important a part in the history of the world." Worms are in fact a gardener's best friend because of the ways they care for the soil. They are commonly known as "nature's plough" because their tunnels allow water and air to pass easily through the soil to the plant roots. Worms eat dead leaves and other plant matter, and as they pull this dead and dried matter into their burrows, they add important nutrients to the depths of the soil. Also, their *castings* (poop) add important nutrients to the soil which are also good for the growth of plants. This soil-building quality is vital to the health of forests, grasslands and gardens worldwide.

DEEP BURROWS Worms are *cold-blooded* which means that their body temperature is the same as their environment. For example, when the air temperature is 70 degrees, their body temperature is also 70 degrees. In winter, when the air temperature is cold, earthworms burrow up to 6 feet deep where soil temperatures remain warm.

SLIME Earthworms coat their bodies in a jelly-like slime which allows them to slide easily through rough and bumpy soil. The slime also coats their tunnel walls preventing them from caving in.

family field guide

PROTECTION

Earthworms are a favorite food for several predators, especially robins and moles. Though they do not have eyes or ears, earthworms can feel vibrations in the soil and are able to move quickly away from danger. They can also sense changes in light, so if they are near the soil surface, they can "see" a shadow as it moves over them. Still, they are easily captured by faster-moving predators.

NON-NATIVES

Most earthworms were brought from Europe to the United States in the 1600-1700s. If they existed in Colorado before the Europeans introduced them, they most likely died out in the ice age about 10,000 years earlier. None of Colorado's earthworm species are *native;* all were introduced to this region from somewhere else.

AFTER THE RAIN

Earthworms are commonly observed above ground following rainstorms. In most cases these worms are not evacuating flooded tunnels to avoid drowning. In fact, earthworms are better able to breath in wet environments than in dry ones. Earthworms live below ground because they need to keep their skin moist. Rather than breathing with lungs, air passes through their moist skin. If their skin dries out, they suffocate. Though moving above ground exposes them to predators, these wet days are opportunities to move easily from place to place without having to dig through the dirt. Brief moments above the soil also provide easy mating opportunities.

Babies Young worms form in the red, bulging sac along the body of the females.

Rain Storms Earthworms are most commonly observed following rain storms.

Earwigs

TYPE FOOD FOOD

Garry Pfaffmann

CLASSIFICATION
Kingdom Animal
Phylum Arthropod
Class Insect
Order *Dermaptera* (Earwigs)
2 species in Colorado; over 1,800 species worldwide.

IDENTIFICATION
Nymph Similar to adults, only smaller.
Adult Long, slender body with a pair of harmless *pincers* at the tail end.

LIFE CYCLE
Incomplete metamorphosis
egg-nymph-adult

FOOD
Nymph Same as adult.
Adult Live or dead insects and live or dead plant matter, especially leaves.

HABITAT
Nymph Same as adult.
Adult Hide beneath leaves, rocks, logs, wood piles and other dark, shady outdoor places. May also hide in small cracks around baseboards in houses.

NAME The name "earwig" originated from an old myth that these bugs commonly crawled into peoples' ears and fed on human brains! Though they like to crawl into small, dark and humid spaces for hiding, they are harmless, not only to your brain, but even to your fingers. The scientific name *Dermaptera* refers to the leathery front wings which look like skin on many earwig species (*derma* is Latin for "skin").

PESTS Earwigs are small and cannot move long distances, but they can quickly crawl up a set of stairs and beneath the crack of an old screen door. Many earwigs crawl indoors following long periods of rain in search of drier conditions. Fortunately they do not usually become long-term household pests because they cannot reproduce indoors. While an individual adult may take shelter in a house, eggs and nymphs cannot survive in dry, indoor environments.

HIBERNATION Earwigs live on or near the soil surface during their active summer months, but in fall, when temperatures drop, they burrow up to six feet below the soil. This depth is safe from freezing temperatures, so their small, fragile bodies are sure to survive winter. As they wake, the females lay eggs in small chambers several inches below the soil. Once the nymphs are able to feed themselves, the family moves back up to the top of the soil for summer feeding.

family field guide

NOCTURNAL

Earwigs are usually observed hiding in dark, shady spaces because they are nocturnal. At night, when most songbirds are asleep, they actively crawl around the ground in search of food, but during the daylight hours when the sun is hot and more winged predators are active, they go into hiding.

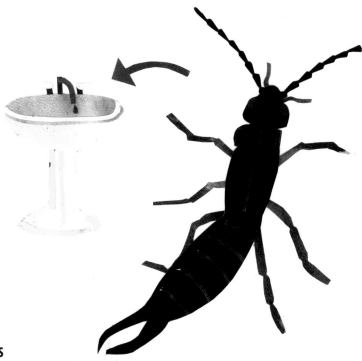

PINCERS

Earwigs are most easily identified by the *pincers* which stick out from their hind end. These pincers look like they could cause a good pinch, but they are harmless to such large creatures as curious children. Though they are too small to hurt people, they act as tools used for catching prey and for defending against insect-predators.

Male Male earwigs have curved pincers which look dangerous but are harmless to human fingers.

Females Females (above) have pincers that are more parallel compared to those of males.

Millipedes

LOOK   TYPE   FOOD

Garry Pfaffmann

CLASSIFICATION

Kingdom Animal
Phylum Arthropod
Class *Diplopoda* (Millipedes)
About 30 species in Colorado; over 10,000 species worldwide.

IDENTIFICATION

Millipede Long, rounded body with two pairs of legs per body segment.

LIFE CYCLE

Incomplete metamorphosis
Millipedes are not insects, but they molt as they grow.

FOOD

Young and Adult Dead plant matter especially dried leaves, wood, roots and fungi.

HABITAT

Young and Adult Dark, moist areas; usually beneath rocks, leaves and logs.

DECOMPOSERS Millipedes only eat dead leaves, rotting wood and other *decaying* matter. Animals, fungi and bacteria that eat all of the dead stuff off the ground are called *decomposers*. Decomposers get energy from dead and dried matter, then cycle these leftovers that other animals cannot eat, back to the soil. If there were no decomposers in the ground, dead leaves, grasses, poop and other materials would build up on the ground and the soil would be buried by tons of wasted material.

DEFENSE Insects and other arthropods are common foods for birds and mammals. Many millipedes defend themselves by producing a smelly oil that makes them taste terrible. After handling some species, people may notice a foul smell on their hands. While some kids may dare each other to eat earthworms, millipedes should never be eaten as they can cause a terrible stomachache!

SOIL DWELLERS Millipedes live in dark, moist environments. Their bodies dry out quickly when exposed to direct sunlight and dry conditions, so they typically hide beneath leaves, rocks and logs which provide shady and humid conditions. They are commonly found beneath rocks and logs because they are nocturnal and are usually resting while children are busy exploring.

family field guide

HOW MANY LEGS?

While the name millipede refers to the number 1,000, the number of legs varies greatly between species and age. As with all arthropods, millipede bodies are segmented. As millipedes molt, they grow more body segments so older animals have longer bodies and more legs than younger ones.

PROTECTION

Though they may have hundreds of legs, millipedes are slow-moving animals. For protection against centipedes and other predators, their body is covered in a hard shell-like material, much like that of the roly-poly.

A YEAR IN THE LIFE

Millipede eggs are usually laid in spring or early summer. They hatch as very small, light colored "worms," but careful observation reveals many tiny legs from the very beginning of their lives. As they grow older, they grow larger and darker and the millipede form becomes easily recognizable. By winter, most millipedes have nearly grown to adulthood before they burrow beneath the soil, often near foundations of houses where temperatures are warm.

Legs Millipedes have two legs per body segment, which seem to move like feathers as they walk.

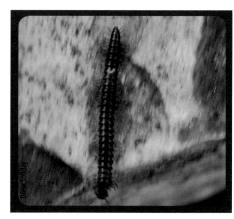

Segments Each bulging section of this millipede's body is called a "segment."

Roly-polies
(Pill bugs)

Garry Pfaffmann

CLASSIFICATION

Kingdom Animal
Phylum Arthropod
Class Crustacean
Order Isopod (roly-polies and sowbugs)
About 20 roly-poly and sowbug species in Colorado; 3,000 species worldwide.

IDENTIFICATION

Young and Adult Seven pairs of legs, segmented body, rolls into a ball when disturbed.

LIFE CYCLE

Incomplete metamorphosis
Roly-polies are not insects, but they molt as they grow.

FOOD

Young and Adult Dead and decaying animal and plant matter including leaves, roots, wood and fungi.

HABITAT

Young and Adult Under rocks, logs or other covered places in gardens, forests and grasslands; need moist soil, but not too wet.

CRUSTACEANS Roly-polies (also called pill bugs) are a *crustacean* which means that they are related to shrimp, crayfish, lobsters and scuds. Only a few crustaceans are able to live on land including roly-polies, sowbugs and wood lice.

TUNNEL BUILDER Like worms, roly-polies help to keep the soil healthy. They dig tiny burrows in the soil as they travel from place to place (usually not more than several square feet). These tunnels allow air and water to pass through the soil. This increased movement of air and water is important for healthy plant growth.

PROTECTION The most entertaining behavior of roly-polies is, of course, their ability to roll up into a ball. This is the reason for their common name, roly-poly. This rolling behavior allows the hard shell, or *cuticle*, to wrap around their soft belly so that it is not exposed to predators. This offers them protection from beetles, centipedes and other *carnivorous* bugs, but obviously does not protect against large predators.

MOISTURE Oxygen enters their body through a tiny hole which leads to their "lungs." This hole cannot close, so water evaporates easily. If the lungs dry out, the roly-poly suffocates. Because their bodies dry out easily and their "lungs" need to stay moist, roly-polies are most often found in damp soils.

family field guide

NAME

Though there are over 3,000 species of roly-polies in the world, the most common in our region is called *Armadillidium vulgare*. The genus name refers to the armadillo, an animal which has a similar shaped "shell" covering the back.

BABIES

Similar to humans, baby roly-polies grow inside a small pouch on the mother's body. Several dozen babies grow for several weeks inside this pouch, then are born into the world looking like small versions of the adults.

SOW BUGS AND ROLY-POLIES

The sowbug is a relative of the roly-poly. They both have seven pairs of legs, the same armored "shell" and live in a similar habitat. Sowbugs however, have two small "tails" on their backside which are absent in roly-polies and sowbugs are unable to roll into tight balls for protection.

Protection Roly-polies are best known for their ability to curl into balls when disturbed.

Young Young roly-polies look similar to adults but are smaller and lighter in color.

family field guide

Spiders

Whitney Cranshaw, Colorado State University, Bugwood.org

CLASSIFICATION

Kingdom Animal
Phylum Arthropod
Class Arachnid
Order *Araneae*
About 600 species in Colorado; about 37,000 species worldwide

IDENTIFICATION

Adult and Young Two distinct body parts, eight legs, three or four pairs of eyes on the head.

LIFE CYCLE

Incomplete metamorphosis
Spiders are not insects, but they molt as they grow.

FOOD

Adult and Young Bugs of all kinds.

HABITAT

Adult and Young Found in all different habitats and ecosystems including houses, boulder fields, alpine tundra, forests, grasslands and more.

SPIDER SILK The common name *spider* comes from a German word meaning "spinner." All spiders can spin silk which may be used for capturing prey, protecting eggs, dispersing young and building safe shelters. The silk produced by spiders is unique in nature. Its *tensile strength* (the amount of pressure that it can absorb before it breaks) is greater than high quality steel. It is also very flexible, so it can stretch significantly before breaking. Equally important, it is very lightweight; it is estimated that a thread of spider's silk wrapped around the earth would weigh less than one pound. Spider's silk is such a remarkable material, scientists continue to study its composition in hopes of using the spider's wisdom and chemistry to improve our own engineering abilities.

PREDATORS All spiders are predators; they capture and eat other bugs. Not all spiders, however, use webs to capture their prey. Some stalk their prey while others ambush their prey as they pass close by. Once the prey is captured, spiders bite them with fangs that inject venom into the body. The venom either paralyzes or kills the prey. Next, they "vomit" chemicals into the prey which turn its insides into liquid. The spider then uses its strong stomach muscles to "vacuum" out the liquified body like a milkshake.

family field guide

TWO BODY PARTS

While insects have three body parts (head, thorax, abdomen), spiders have only two. The head and thorax are joined together (the eyes and legs are both located on this front part) and, as with insects, the abdomen contains the organs for reproduction, digestion and excretion.

POISONOUS SPIDERS

All spiders are poisonous in the sense that they all produce venom which is used to capture and kill prey. Of the 37,000 species of spiders in the world, only a handful are of much danger to humans. The most dangerous spider in Colorado is the Western Black Widow (*pictured p. 54)* which frequents dry, warm environments and is not common in mountain ecosystems.

DADDY LONGLEGS: NOT A SPIDER AT ALL!

The name Daddy Longlegs is commonly used to describe two different bugs. The name most often refers to a bug called a Harvestman, which is an arachnid, but not a spider at all (see page 44). Look carefully at the body of the "Daddy Longlegs" which you are observing; if it has one body part, it is a Harvestman. If it has two distinct body parts it is likely a Cellar Spider (*below right*). This is indeed a spider which commonly hangs from its unorganized web in cellars and other lightly visited areas of the home. Though spiders are not much appreciated inside most peoples' homes, these are one of the best caretakers for controlling insect populations as they eat most any bug and have very few enemies (besides vacuum cleaners).

Webs Most, but not all, spiders use webs to catch prey. Many species are hunters or ambushers. This web pattern is created by many species of orb spiders.

Long Legs The head of the Daddy Longlegs Spider (a Cellar Spider) looks quite different from the true Daddy Longlegs (*see p. 44*).

Gall Makers

HABITAT

LIFE CYCLE

LIFE CYCLE

LOOK

TYPE

Garry Pfaffmann

CLASSIFICATION

Kingdom Animal

Phylum Arthropod

Class Insect

Order varies; wasps (*hymenoptera*) and flies (*diptera*) are most common.

IDENTIFICATION

The insects are not likely to be seen. Instead, look for unusual shaped growths on plants; these are the galls in which the insect larvae live.

LIFE CYCLE

Varies, but the nymphs or larvae of all grow inside the gall, then the adult hatches and lives among plants.

FOOD

Nymph and Larva Feed on the plant material inside the gall.

Adults Varies, but many eat the leaves or other parts of the host plant or neighboring plants.

HABITAT

Varies, but all galls are on plants; some grow from leaves, others from stems.

WHAT IS A GALL? A *gall* is an obvious and unique growth on plants that acts as a nest for many different types of insects. These unusual growths are produced when insects inject their saliva into the plant. The saliva acts as a chemical which "tells" the plant to grow in a certain way. The plant follows the instructions and the plant grows these unique, hollow features. The tiny nymphs grow inside the protection of the gall, safe from wind, rain, cold and most predators.

MANY INSECTS Galls come in many different shapes and sizes and form on a variety of plants. Each different gall is made by a different type of insect. Many species of wasps, flies, mites and aphids use galls in their immature stages of growth.

COOLEY SPRUCE GALL These obvious galls (pictured above) grow on the tips of spruce branches and look like brown pineapples among the green needles. They are often mistaken as a cluster of dead needles, but these hard, prickly galls are made by an *aphid* (a tiny little plant eating insect), the Cooley Spruce Gall Aphid. Female aphids survive winter under the tree bark. They lay eggs in spring, then the newly hatched aphid nymphs feed on the new needles. Their saliva causes a gall to form. The nymphs then move inside the gall through the summer. Once full-grown, the adults fly out of the gall and feed on Douglas Fir needles.

family field guide

POPLAR TWIGGALL

A fly produces these galls on the stems of aspen and cottonwood twigs.

ROSE HIPS?

A gall wasp forms this red growth on the branches of wild rose bushes. The galls look similar to rose hips, the berries which form on rose plants in late summer.

OAK LEAF GALLS

These red blister-like galls are produced by a wasp.

WILLOW CONE GALL

A midge (similar to a fly) forms its cone-shaped galls on the branches of willow bushes.

Leaves Some galls form from saliva injected into leaves. Larvae grow inside these hollow "nests."

Stems Stems injected by gall-making insects often form interesting shapes.

Grasshoppers

HABITAT   **LIFE CYCLE**

LOOK   **TYPE**   **FOOD**

Garry Pfaffmann

CLASSIFICATION

Kingdom Animal
Phylum Arthropod
Class Insect
Order *Orthoptera* (grasshoppers and crickets)
Family *Acrididae*
145 species in Colorado; 10,000 species worldwide.

IDENTIFICATION

Young and Adult   Huge back legs for jumping, obvious eyes, short antennae, hard shell and wings.

LIFE CYCLE

Incomplete metamorphosis
Egg-nymph-adult

FOOD

Young and Adult All grasshoppers eat leaves. Some prefer grasses, others larger leaves, but most species prefer specific leafy foods. May eat other grasshoppers!

HABITAT

Varies between species; common from lowlands to alpine tundra wherever plants are available.

POPULATION CONTROL   Because grasshoppers feed mostly on leaves of plants, large populations can cause big problems for farmers. Only a few species within Colorado have reached such high populations that they have destroyed food crops dramatically, but when these species swarm on a field, they can be a farmer's worst nightmare! This is a good example of why population controls are important in ecosystems. Flies, birds, wasps, beetles and rodents eat grasshoppers and spring rains often kill many young nymphs. These are some of nature's controls to help keep grasshopper populations within healthy limits.

SPITTING INSECT   Some grasshopper species spit a brown liquid when disturbed (you may notice this if you catch one in your hands). This liquid is called *tobacco juice*, though it is not related to tobacco in any way. In fact, these disturbed hoppers are throwing-up some of the contents from their stomach as a way to scare you, a potential predator. Imagine, if a bunch of bullies try to bother you on the playground and you throw up all over their shoes; they are likely to turn and walk away....some of the time!

HOPPING   Grasshoppers' powerful legs are always cocked and ready to jump. They can jump 20 times the length of their body with the help of their wings. Imagine a third grader jumping the entire length of a basketball court, from a standing position!

family field guide

EGGS

Female grasshoppers burrow their "tails" beneath the soil and drop their eggs just below the surface. Bundles of 10-50 rice-sized eggs are dropped all at one time. Certain flies are able to identify these egg clusters and they choose to lay their eggs near those of the hoppers'. The flies often hatch first and use the grasshopper eggs as food.

CRACKLING WINGS

Besides having strong legs for jumping, most grasshoppers use their wings to give added distance to their escape. The stiff wings of some species make a loud crackling sound when they beat against each other in flight.

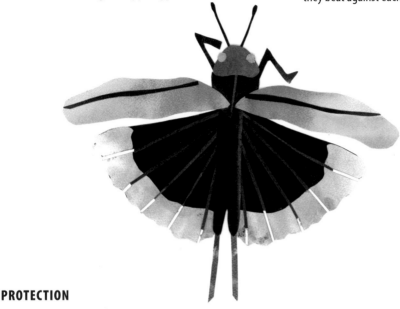

PROTECTION

Grasshoppers are designed with protection in mind. Most species are very well camouflaged into grassy landscapes with green and brown colors. Such camouflage allows them to hide from predators. When danger approaches, their first response is to drop from a plant into the tall grasses where they can hide. If they are in short grass or rocks, they use their powerful legs and wings to jump toward safety.

Feet Grasshoppers have claws and sticky pads which help them climb vertical surfaces.

Camouflage Most grasshoppers are colored in a way that allows them to blend into their habitat.

Ladybugs

HABITAT   **LIFE CYCLE**

LOOK   **TYPE**   **FOOD**

© Pfaffmann

CLASSIFICATION
Kingdom Animal
Phylum Arthropod
Class Insect
Order *Coleoptera* (Beetles)
Family *Coccinellidae* (Ladybugs)
About 80 species in Colorado; over 5,000 species worldwide.

IDENTIFICATION
Larva Flattened, soft body; black with orange spotting; six obvious legs.
Pupa Rounder soft body, usually orange.
Adult Rounded body with hard wing covers; usually has orange and black patterns.

LIFE CYCLE
Complete metamorphosis
egg-larva-pupa-adult

FOOD
Larva and Adult Small plant-eating insects; especially *aphids*.

HABITAT
Larva and Adult On plants where plant-eating insects are present.

CARNIVORES   Ladybugs are a type of beetle that feeds almost entirely on other insects. Aphids, a tiny bug that lives on and eats plants, are their favorite food, but ladybugs eat other small insects, too. Female ladybugs lay their eggs within a colony of aphids so that when the larvae are born, they do not have to travel to find food. Each ladybug larva eats several hundred aphids within a couple of weeks, and continues to eat them as they grow into adulthood. Gardeners commonly use ladybugs as a natural way of killing insects that can harm their plants.

PROTECTION   Bright colorful patterns are often a signal of *toxicity*, or posion, among many types of animals, including insects. In this way, the colorful patterns on a ladybug's back act as defense against predators. Ladybugs are, in fact, poisonous, but a human would have to eat several hundred before becoming ill. Besides their color, ladybugs also release a yellow, smelly, oil from their legs when disturbed. The stink usually causes curious predators to leave them alone.

UNIQUE FEATURES Ladybugs are not all alike. Though they are most easily identified by their orange, red or yellow wing covers with dark spots, different species have varying numbers of spots, different colored wing guards and different color patterns on their heads. Some ladybugs even have grey or black wing covers and are difficult to identify as ladybugs at all.

family field guide

WING COVERS

The brightly colored back of most ladybugs is a pair of hard, shell-like covers which protect the wings. In flight, the ladybug moves these wing covers (*elytra*) out of the way so that the transparent wings underneath can flap freely.

MANY NAMES

Ladybugs are commonly called Lady Beetles because they are a type of beetle. In Europe, they are called Ladybirds.

WINTER

In winter, ladybugs huddle together in large colonies beneath bark, in abandoned barns and other protected areas where they hibernate through cold temperatures. These colorful bugs cannot fly when temperatures drop below 55 degrees, so when the long cold season begins, they find a protected place and their bodies slow down until warmer temperatures arrive.

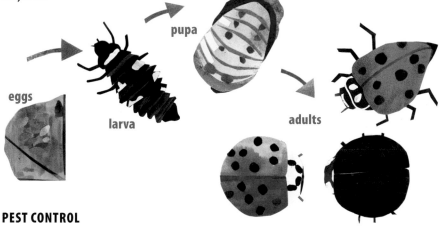

eggs

larva

pupa

adults

PEST CONTROL

A common ladybug in North America (*Coccinella septempunctata*) was brought from Europe to the United States by farmers to control insect pests. This species has seven black spots on its orange wing covers (*sept* is latin for seven) and is the official insect of Delaware, Massachusetts, New Hampshire, Pennsylvania, Ohio and Tennessee. While most ladybugs are known for their helpful pest control, some species have become pests including the Mexican Bean Beetle.

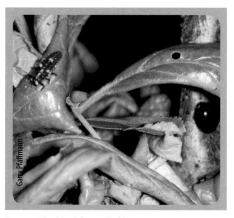

Larva The black larva (left) soon enters its pupa phase then emerges as an adult (right).

Wing Covers The colorful wing covers (*elytra*) protect the wings which are hiding underneath.

Slugs
(Garden Slugs)

Garry Pfaffmann

HABITAT

LIFE CYCLE

LOOK

TYPE

FOOD

CLASSIFICATION
Kingdom Animal
Phylum Mollusk
Class Gastropod (snails and slugs)
Order *Pulmonata* (land slugs and snails)
About 40 land slug species in North America; about 25,000 species worldwide.

IDENTIFICATION
Adult and Young Soft body, two obvious tentacles; look like snails without the obvious shell.

LIFE CYCLE
No metamorphosis
Slugs are not insects and do not molt.

FOOD
Adult and Young Garden slugs eat leaves.

HABITAT
Adult and Young Live in wet, shady areas; they often hide under leaves and forest litter during the day, then come out at night to feed.

SLOW AS A SLUG Slugs are *mollusks*, not insects. They are more closely related to squids, snails and clams than to ants and beetles. A common feature among all mollusks is their "foot." Though mollusks do not have legs, they all move by suctioning a large "foot" to the ground, then using it as an anchor to extend their body forward. The body extends, the foot suctions and the rest of the body creeps forward again. This movement is very slow and is the reason for the saying, "slow as a slug."

SLUG SLIME Wherever a slug moves, it leaves a trail of slime in its path (see photo at right). This trail can be followed by other slugs that may want to share food. It can also be followed the next day by the same slug as a guide back to the feeding plant. Slugs' bodies are entirely covered in slime, a characteristic that makes them very slippery and difficult for predators to catch (try holding onto a greased watermelon in a swimming pool).

DEATH BY SALT It is common knowledge that pouring salt on a slug causes a quick death. The salt pulls water outward from their soft bodies causing them to dehydrate and die. The same outcome occurs if they stay out in the daytime sun; the warm, dry air pulls water outward causing them to dehydrate. For this reason slugs usually hide in moist shady areas throughout the day, then come out to feed at night.

GASTROPODS

Slugs belong to a classification of animals called *Gastropods*. The word *gastro* is Latin for mouth, and *pod* is Latin for foot. All animals in this group have a foot used for moving and all have a mouth located on that foot.

DRUNK AS A SLUG

Slugs are considered pests in most gardens. People spend many hours trying to stop slugs from eating their lettuce leaves, cabbage heads and other leafy vegetables. One of the most successful ways of trapping slugs is by placing a shallow container filled with beer on the garden floor. Slugs are attracted to fermenting grains, an important ingredient in beer. They are not attracted to the alcohol! The slugs like the smell of the beer, so they slide into the mini swimming pool where they drown. It's a sad way to go, but a garden can only feed so many mouths, right?

Slugs are closely related to snails, a similar looking animal with a large, easy-to-identify shell. Though slugs have nearly lost these shells after millions of years of evolution, a tiny shell still remains on their backs, but it is hidden beneath a layer of skin making it invisible. The part of their back where the mini-shell grows is called the *mantle*.

BREATHING HOLE

Notice the tiny hole on the slug's side *(pictured p. 62)*. This hole allows air to pass in and out of "lungs" as they breath. The hole cannot close entirely, so slugs must live in moist environments or their lungs will dry out and they will suffocate.

Slug Food Slugs eat holes in plants (including potatoes), making them a pest for most gardeners.

Slime Trail Slugs leave a pathway of slime as they move, creating a trail for others to follow.

Spittlebugs

HABITAT　　**LIFE CYCLE**

LOOK　　**TYPE**　　**FOOD**

Garry Pfaffmann

CLASSIFICATION

Kingdom Animal
Phylum Arthropod
Class Insect
Order *Hemiptera* (True Bugs)
Family *Cercopidae*
At least 15 species in Colorado; 850 species worldwide.

IDENTIFICATION

Nymphs Most notably, the nymphs are found inside a bubbly mass of "spittle." Colors vary from green, then grow to yellow, then to brown.
Adult Similar size to the nymph, but darker and with wings.

LIFE CYCLE

Incomplete metamorphosis
egg-nymph-adult

FOOD

Larva and Adult Sap from leafy plants.

HABITAT

Larva and Adult Juniper Spittlebugs on juniper trees; Meadow Spittlebugs on grasses and other plants in sunny meadows or gardens.

MAKING SPITTLE Spittlebugs get their name from the bubbly, frothy, watery mass which the nymphs create as a hiding place. The bubbly "spittle" is created by sucking large amounts of watery sap out of the host plant, then pushing it out their back side. As they force the sap out, they wag their tail up and down which helps to froth the mixture. This is similar to a coffee maker forcing hot air into milk and bobbing it up and down to make it frothy. As the bubbly mass is formed, the bug uses its hind legs to cover its body.

WHY SPITTLE? The formation of spittle-masses provides several important life-supporting functions for the nymphs. First, the spittle provides hiding. Once covered in the bubbly mass, predators cannot easily see the bugs and most are not likely to dive head-first into a mass of bubbles without knowing what is inside. Second, the bubbles act as temperature control. Even on very hot days, the watery bubbles create a cool *microclimate*, protecting the nymphs from the heat. Finally, the bubbles prevent water loss from the spittlebug's body, an important factor for survival in all *arthropods*. Living in a watery world is a clever way of keeping the body moist. While roly-polies and centipedes hide under rocks to keep moist and cool, spittlebugs alter their habitat so that they can beat the heat and the dryness without being stuck under a rock!

family field guide

LIFE CYCLE

Only young spittlebug nymphs form spittle masses. A nymph lives in its spittle until it molts its skin, then it moves and forms a new spittle mass in a different location. After molting five times on five different plants, the bug grows to adulthood. Adult spittlebugs, called froghoppers do not use the protection of spittle. They die in winter, but their eggs survive on the stems where they are laid.

WORLD RECORD HOLDER

Adult spittlebugs are called froghoppers and are rarely observed because they jump a great distance when danger approaches. Scientists have identified them as the longest-jumping family of insects in the world. While they are only ⅕-inch tall, they can jump more than 2 feet in the air without the assistance of wings. If a 5' tall person was to jump in a similar proportion, she would be able to jump 700 feet in the air, taller than a 70-story building...without wings!

DOES IT HURT?

Spittlebugs use plant sap both to make their spittle and as food. They poke their tiny needle-like mouth into the plant and suck out the juices which move from the roots up to the leaves. Their sucking habit causes plants to grow smaller and produce fewer flowers, but is not likely to kill the host plant. Ranchers and other agriculture professionals consider spittlebugs as pests because they slow plant production.

Names Immature nymphs are called *spittlebugs*. Adults (pictured above) are called *froghoppers*.

Spittle Spittlebug nymphs hide in a watery froth of sap which they create for protection.

family field guide

Tent Caterpillars

HABITAT   **LIFE CYCLE**   **LOOK**

TYPE   **IMMATURE**   **ADULT**

Whitney Cranshaw, Colorado State, Bugwood.org

CLASSIFICATION

Kingdom Animal
Phylum Arthropod
Class Insect
Order *Lepidoptera* (butterflies and moths)
Family *Lasiocampidae*
10 species in Colorado; 1,500 species worldwide.

IDENTIFICATION

Larva Caterpillars with long hairs.
Pupa Large, silky cocoon.
Adult Varies, but all emerge as moths.

LIFE CYCLE

Complete metamorphosis
egg-larva-pupa-adult

FOOD

Larva Leaves.
Adult The moths eat nectar and other sweet liquids.

HABITAT

Larva Within the silken tent among branches of tall trees. Tree varieties vary among species.
Adult Moths hide among plants during the day and feed at night.

SILKEN TENTS Tent caterpillars are the silk-spinning, tent-making larvae of several varieties of moths. Unlike spiders which use their silk to catch prey, these tents are used to provide protection against predators. Large colonies of caterpillars rest inside the safety of the netting throughout the day, then leave the tent to feed at night.

DIVERSITY Tent-making caterpillars are identified by the tent making season and by the trees in which they are built. Western Tent Caterpillars are the most commonly observed species in spring and early summer. Their tents fill the branches of Aspen, Cottonwood and other deciduous trees. Sonoran Tent Caterpillars build similar tents in Gambel Oak shrubs, also in spring and early summer. Forest Tent Caterpillars also produce huge colonies, but they do not produce a large tent. Instead, they form a mat of silk on the tree trunk so they can stick to the tree's bark.

PROTECTION Western Tent Caterpillars use their tents for safety while resting in mid-day and while molting. While feeding, however, they must leave the tent at which time they are vulnerable to birds and other predators. For added safety, their bodies have tiny hairs which irritate most predators and prevent them from eating the squishy caterpillars.

family field guide

TRAILS

Tent caterpillars can only see about ¼-inch in front of their eyes which makes long-distance travel difficult. In response, they leave a trail of silk when they leave the tent to feed, then they follow the silken string back to the safety of the tent so that they do not get lost. Also, their silk has a unique smell which allows them to distinguish between their silk and that of a spider's web so that they do not get trapped.

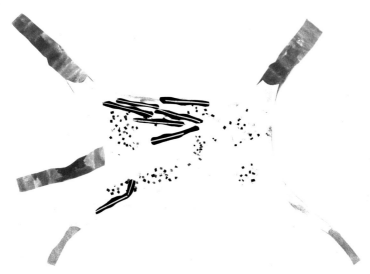

SURVIVING THE COLD

Western Tent Caterpillars lay eggs in mid-summer. The caterpillars develop inside the egg, but must survive the winter before they hatch in spring. During these cold months, their bodies are filled with *glycerol*, a chemical similar to antifreeze which is used in cars. This chemical prevents them from freezing during cold temperatures.

POPULATION CONTROL

Flies and other parasitic insects lay their eggs on caterpillars' bodies while they are out feeding. When these insects hatch inside the caterpillars, the tiny larvae eat and kill the caterpillars. Parasitic insects are the most important predators in controlling tent caterpillar populations.

Adult Tent caterpillars are moth larvae. Adults emerge like this western tent caterpillar adult.

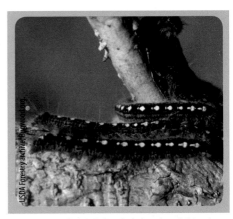

Hairs Tent caterpillars are covered with long hairs which deter birds and other predators.

Ticks

Scott Bauer, USDA

HABITAT

LIFE CYCLE

LOOK

TYPE

FOOD

CLASSIFICATION

Kingdom Animal
Phylum Arthropod
Class Arachnid
Order *Acari*
Family *Ixodidae*
13 species in Colorado; 850 species worldwide.

IDENTIFICATION

Nymph Small versions of the adult, but with only six legs.
Adult Flat, rounded body with eight legs.

LIFE CYCLE

Incomplete metamorphosis
egg-nymph-adult

FOOD

Nymph and Adult Blood from host animals.

HABITAT

Nymph and Adult Among tall grasses and shrubs, usually in lower mountain elevations.

BLOOD SUCKERS Ticks feed entirely on the blood of larger animals. As they suck the blood from these *hosts*, their bodies fill with blood and they grow tremendously. A tick may feed for up to a week before releasing itself, after which their body weight may increase by 100 times (imagine walking into a restaurant weighing 50 pounds and walking out weighing 5,000!).

HOSTS The animals that ticks feed from are called *hosts*. Rodents, deer, cows, birds and people are all common hosts which provide blood for ticks. Dogs are also common hosts, so be sure to check yourself and your pets after hiking in tall grasses and shrubs.

FINDING FOOD Ticks are not able to jump or fly, so they can only attach to host animals that touch them. Ticks climb to the tips of grasses or shrubs waiting for an animal to brush up against the plant. They are very sensitive to heat and to carbon dioxide (the gas that animals exhale as they breath). At the slightest increase in temperature or carbon dioxide, they wave their legs outward from the plant in hopes of grabbing onto a passing animal (see photo at right). This behavior is called *questing*. Once contact is made, they grab onto the animal and climb onto its skin. Because it may take a long time for animals to pass through their environment, ticks can go months or even a full year without eating!

family field guide

DISEASE

Ticks often carry diseases and pass them onto the animals they bite. Lyme Disease is a dangerous illness passed by ticks and, though it is common in many parts of the United States, it is not common in the Rocky Mountain region. Colorado Tick Fever is the most common disease passed by ticks in the Rocky Mountain region and its symptoms are similar to the flu. Though Rocky Mountain Spotted Fever was first identified in the Rocky Mountains, it is most common along the east coast.

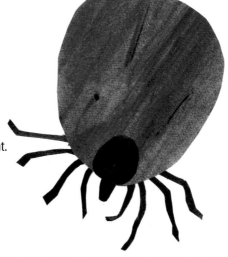

ENGORGED

After a week's feeding, a fully *engorged* tick looks like a grape with tiny legs sticking out the front.

LIFE CYCLE

Some of the most common ticks have a "three-host life cycle" which means that they feed on three different animals during their lifetime. To begin, eggs hatch as six-legged nymphs which must attach to passing animals, suck their blood then drop to the ground. On the ground, they molt into eight-legged nymphs which look very similar to adults, but are not yet able to reproduce. The nymphs must attach to a second animal, suck their blood, then drop to the ground again where they molt into adults which are able to reproduce. The adult must attach to a third animal, suck the blood, mate, then drop to the ground again before eggs can be laid. Males usually mate with a female while she is feeding on her final host, then the males die soon after.

Questing Ticks stretch their front legs outward from their perch waiting to attach to a passing host.

Engorged As ticks suck blood from their hosts, their bodies' grow to 100 times their normal size.

Bees

HABITAT   HABITAT   LIFE CYCLE

LOOK   TYPE   ADULT

John Severns

CLASSIFICATION

Kingdom Animal
Phylum Arthropod
Class Insect
Order *Hymenoptera* (ants, bees and wasps)
At least 1,000 bee species in Colorado;
30,000 species worldwide.

IDENTIFICATION

Adults Hairs on back, thicker body than
wasps (wasps have a thin waist between
body segments).

LIFE CYCLE

Complete metamorphosis
egg-larva-pupa-adult

FOOD

Larva Honey and pollen.
Adult Nectar and pollen in spring and summer, honey when flowers are not in bloom.

HABITAT

Bumble bees and honey bees build hives
in hollow logs or stumps; digger bees live
individually in burrows on the ground;
leafcutter bees nest individually in tunnels
within rotting wood.

BEE VARIETIES Bumble bees and honey bees are
the most commonly recognized bees. Both have hairs
on their backs and live in group hives. The majority of
bee species, however, live alone. Over 170 different
Colorado species live individually in burrows which
they dig in the soil. Nearly 80 species of leafcutter
bees nest individually in tunnels of rotting wood. They
cut dime-sized pieces from leaves and line their tunnels with these leaf cuttings. All bees, whether hive
builder, soil digger or leaf cutter, eat pollen and nectar
and feed pollen and honey to their young.

POLLEN AND NECTAR During summer months, bees
eat nectar and pollen from flowers. Bumble bees and
honey bees send out *workers* to collect the food and
bring it back to the hive to feed the rest of the bee colony. Worker bees "chew" the nectar then store it in the
honey comb. As the water evaporates from the nectar,
it turns to honey. Honey bees make more honey than
other bees because they use it as a winter food supply
(all other bees hibernate through winter).

GENTLE BUZZ Bees only sting when protecting their
hive or nest, or if they are being threatened. They
are not aggressive like wasps. Ninety percent of "bee
stings" are actually wasp stings. Bees do not "want"
to sting. In fact, they die soon after their stinger is
removed.

family field guide

SWARMING

In spring and late summer it is not uncommon to hear swarms of thousands of bees flying overhead. This only occurs when a hive of bees becomes so large that it decides to split. The queen and thousands of its worker bees (unproductive females) and drones (males) leave the hive and move to create a new hive. Thousands of bees remain behind and feed one of the larvae a special nutrient-rich food called "royal jelly" so that it can grow larger and become productive. This new larva will grow to be the new queen of the original hive. Swarming bees are usually harmless unless disturbed.

WINTER

Honey bees are the only bee which remains active through winter. They do not fly out of their hives during these frozen months, but their activity within the hive is enough to keep them warm.

HUMAN FOOD

The importance of bees in ecosystems is often underappreciated. Every seed-producing plant on earth needs pollen from a different plant of the same species to be transferred onto its female parts so that it can form a seed. For example, before apples can grow, the trees' flowers must be pollinated in spring. Because bees eat pollen and nectar, they are the most important insects in moving pollen from flower to flower. Farmers of many crops depend heavily on a healthy bee population for their crops to grow!

Honey Bee Honey bees carry pollen back to the hive in *pollen baskets* on their hind legs.

Pollination As a bee searches for nectar, pollen grains dust its body and flowers are pollinated.

Butterflies

LOOK

TYPE

IMMATURE

ADULT

CLASSIFICATION

Kingdom Animal
Phylum Arthropod
Class Insect
Order *Lepidoptera* (butterflies and moths)
Over 200 species in Colorado; about 20,000 worldwide.

IDENTIFICATION

Larva Caterpillars of many different color patterns, but all are worm-like.
Pupa Hide in *chrysalises* of varying shapes and colors.
Adult Long, slender body, four wings, antennae have a "club" at the tip.

LIFE CYCLE

Complete metamorphosis
egg-larva-pupa-adult

FOOD

Larva Most species eat only leaves.
Adult Flower nectar, sap and other sweet liquids.

HABITAT

Larva In trees and among other leafy plants.
Adult Varies greatly among species.

WINGS The Latin name *Lepidoptera* means "scale wing." After touching a butterfly wing, a "powder" rubs off of it. This powder is actually hundreds of scales which rub off when touched. The colors in butterfly wings are created by these tiny scales. If all of the scales are rubbed off, the wing looks transparent with intricate vein patterns, similar to a dragonfly's wing. Butterflies can still fly after scales are removed, as long as the wings are not bent or broken.

BUTTERFLIES AND MOTHS Butterflies and moths are easily confused. Generally, butterflies close their wings while at rest, while most moths spread their wings flat. Butterflies are usually active during the day while moths are more active at night. Butterflies have a club-shaped tip on their antennae, while moths do not.

CATERPILLARS Caterpillars are immature butterflies. They are the eating and growing phase of the butterfly life cycle. They eat more leaves than just about any other animal, in proportion to their size. They are not able to mate or lay eggs. As they grow, caterpillars *molt* several times, similar to the way a snake sheds its skin. A chemical in their bodies tells them when it is time to form a *chrysalis* (moths form *cocoons*). Within the chrysalis, the caterpillar grows wings, antennae and all other adult features before emerging as an adult butterfly.

family field guide

What They Eat and Where

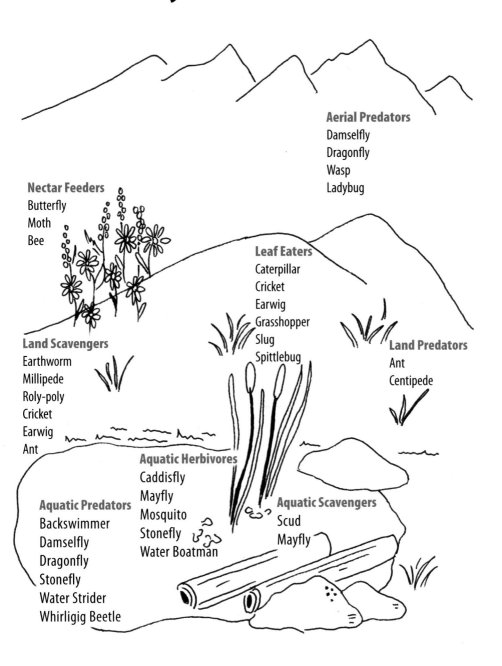

Aerial Predators
Damselfly
Dragonfly
Wasp
Ladybug

Nectar Feeders
Butterfly
Moth
Bee

Leaf Eaters
Caterpillar
Cricket
Earwig
Grasshopper
Slug
Spittlebug

Land Scavengers
Earthworm
Millipede
Roly-poly
Cricket
Earwig
Ant

Land Predators
Ant
Centipede

Aquatic Herbivores
Caddisfly
Mayfly
Mosquito
Stonefly
Water Boatman

Aquatic Scavengers
Scud
Mayfly

Aquatic Predators
Backswimmer
Damselfly
Dragonfly
Stonefly
Water Strider
Whirligig Beetle

family field guide

Award Winners

Weight Gain/Weight Loss: Tick

In a single week-long feeding, ticks drink so much blood that their body size can increase over 100 times in weight. After they digest the blood, they shrink back down to their original size.

Amazing Eyes: Dragonfly

Dragonflies' eyes are made up of many different lenses working together. While humans have one lens in each eye, dragonflies can have up to 30,000 lenses in each eye.

Killer Insect: Mosquito

Mosquitoes cause more human suffering than any other animal on earth. In the U.S., they are carriers of West Nile virus which rarely kills people, but many birds and mammals die from this disease. Throughout the world, it is estimated that 1,000,000 people die every year from diseases passed by mosquitoes.

Earth Digger: Earthworm

Earthworms are recognized as the most important mover of soil in the world. An acre of soil may contain 50,000-1,000,000 earthworms, depending on many conditions. It is estimated that a healthy population of earthworms can move up to 30,000 pounds of soil in a single season.

Food Maker: Honey Bee

It is estimated that honey bees, pollinate $1/3$ of all of our food supply. That means that without honey bees, $1/3$ of all of our food would not grow. This includes all fruits, vegetables, nuts and even hamburger…cows eat grasses which are pollinated by bees, too!

family field guide

Award Winners

Fastest Growing: Caterpillar

Caterpillars grow at a faster rate than any other animal in the world. From the time they hatch from an egg to the time they are ready to build a chrysalis, many caterpillars can increase their body weight by 27,000 times. Imagine a 7 pound baby growing to be 189,000 pound teenager.

Leaf Eater: Caterpillar

Because they grow so much in a single season (see above), caterpillars have to eat a lot of food. Caterpillars are eating machines! As a group, caterpillars eat more leaves each season than any other type of animal.

Insect Migration: Monarch butterfly

Every year, Monarch butterflies hibernate through the winter in the southern U.S. and Mexico. After waking in spring, they fly over 2,000 miles to their mating sites in the northern U.S and Canada. The adults that wintered in Mexico die, but their babies return to Mexico, without anyone showing them the route!

Longest Leaper: Spittlebug

Adult spittlebugs are called froghoppers or treehoppers because of their jumping ability. They are known as the highest jumpers of any animal in the world. This 6mm ($1/5$-inch) tall insect can jump up to 28 inches in the air without any help from wings. Imagine a 5-foot tall person jumping 700 feet in the air from a standing position!

Pest Control: Ladybug

Though they are one of the first insects that children come to love because of their delicate beauty, ladybugs are one of the most important carnivores in the insect world. A single ladybug eats millions of plant-eating insects each season and are a farmer's best friend for controlling insect pests in gardens and pastures.

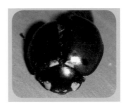

Butterfly Pictures

Black Swallowtail

Painted Lady

Blue Copper (Gossamer)

Cabbage White

Variegated Fritilary

Field Crescent

Orange Sulphur

Red Admiral

Mourning Cloak

Gray Comma

Pine White

Clouded Sulphur

family field guide

Weidemeyer's Admiral

Checkered White

American Lady

Tawney-edged Skipper

Western Swallowtail

Monarch

Northern Crescent

Gorgone Checkerspot

Pale Swallowtail

West Coast Lady

Coral Hairstreak

Pearl Crescent

family field guide

Moth Pictures

family field guide

Glossary

Abdomen The hind segment of an insect which contains the digestive and reproductive organs.

Antennae Two delicate organs attached at the head of insects, crustaceans and other animals; usually their main sense organs. Antennae is plural for antenna.

Anticoagulant A chemical that stops the clotting of blood.

Aphid A very small insect that feeds by sucking sap from plants.

Aquatic insects Any insect that lives part or all of its life in water.

Arachnid A group of invertebrates which includes spiders, scorpions, mites and ticks. Arachnids have four pairs of legs.

Arthropod A group of animals that has no spinal chord, including insects, spiders and crustaceans. All arthropods have a hard exoskeleton that is molted as it grows.

Carnivorous An animal that eats other animals.

Castings Undigested materials, soil, and bacteria excreted by a worm. Worm poop.

Chrysalis The smooth outer covering of a butterfly pupa. The term chrysalis sometimes refers to the pupa itself.

Cocoon The silk covering that protects a moth pupa.

Cerci (singular cercus) A pair of feelers on the tail end of many arthropods. They are often sensory organs and may also be used as weapons or during mating.

Classification Organizing living things based on their common characteristics.

Cold-blooded An animal whose body temperature is similar to the temperature of their environment. All arthropods are cold-blooded.

Complete metamorphosis Four-stage metamorphosis in insect development: egg, nymph, pupa, adult.

Compound eye Thousands of tiny lenses that work together to form one eye; usually creates a broad field of vision.

Crustacean Aquatic arthropods that have a segmented body, an exoskeleton, and paired, jointed limbs. Lobsters, crabs, shrimp and scuds are all crustaceans. Roly-polies are a unique land-living crustacean.

Cuticle The hard, protective outer layer of insects and other arthropods. Also called the exoskeleton.

Decay When leaves, wood or other materials rot and break down to their smallest parts.

Decomposer Organisms that eat dead plant or animal matter, causing them to break down to become part of the soil.

Drone Males within a colony of insects used only for reproduction with the queen.

Elytra The fancy name for the hard wing coverings on a ladybug.

Engorged To fill excessively with blood.

Entomology The study of insects.

Ephemeral Lasting only a short time; short-lived.

Exoskeleton The hard, outer layer that provides support and protection in insects and other arthropods.

Gall Unusual growths on a plant caused by insects; can act as a shelter for developing nymphs or larvae.

Glycerol A natural chemical present in many arthropods that helps to prevent them from freezing during the winter; it acts similar to antifreeze in a car.

Gyrinidal A bad-smelling chemical produced by whirligig beetles; used as protection.

Hatch A large number of aquatic insects all emerging from the water as adults at the same time.

Head The first segment of an insect's body which contains eyes, antennae and mouthparts.

Histamine A chemical released by the immune system during an allergic reaction, causes swelling and inflammation.

Honeydo A sweet tasting liquid produced by some insects.

Host An animal or plant that is food for a parasite; it does not benefit and is often harmed.

Imago The adult stage of an insect.

Immature An animal that is not yet able to reproduce.

Incomplete metamorphosis Three-stage metamorphosis in arthropod growth: egg, larva, adult.

Indicator species A species whose presence or absence provides information on the overall condition of an ecosystem.

Infestation The presence of a very large number of insects or other pests.

Larva (plural: larvae). The immature form of an insect that undergoes complete metamorphosis. Insect larvae look very different from the adult form.

Metamorphosis The process of changing from one form to another. In insects, from the larval stage to the pupal stage to the reproductive adult stage.

Microclimate The climate of a small area such as a cave, house, city or valley that may be different from that in the general region.

Mollusk A group of animals with soft bodies, such as slugs, clams and snails. Most have a hard shell.

Molt Shedding of the exoskeleton before entering another stage of growth.

Myrmecophilous relationship A relationship between ants and other plants or animals.

Native A plant or animal that has always existed in a region; it was not imported from somewhere else.

Nymph The immature form of an insect that undergoes incomplete metamorphosis. Insect nymphs look similar to the adult form. Nymphs never enter the pupal phase.

Omnivore Any animal that eats both plants and meat.

Osmeterium A gland located near the head of some caterpillars which sprays a foul-smelling chemical.

Ovipositor A tube-like structure at the tail of some female insects used to deposit eggs.

Pheromones Chemicals sprayed by some animals which are used as a means of communication.

Pincers Two jaw-like structures which clasp together while holding an object or prey animal.

Pollen baskets Structures on the hind legs of honey bees used for holding pollen while in flight.

Proboscis The "beak" of many insects used to probe and gather food.

Pupa (plural: pupae) The stage of development between the larva and the adult in insects with complete metamorphosis. This stage is usually inactive and no feeding occurs.

Pupal Phase The phase when an insect is inactive as it develops from a larva to an adult.

Queen The reproductive female within a colony of insects including ants, bees and wasps. Her only function in the colony is to make babies.

Raft The gathering of many insects in close formation on water.

Retreat The name of the shell-like casing created by caddisflies.

Scavenger An animal that feeds on dead plants or animals.

Subimago A unique stage in mayflies in which the animal has wings, but is not yet able to reproduce.

Thorax An insect's body is divided into three segments. The thorax is the middle segment and holds the legs and wings.

Toxicity An amount of poison within a material.

Worker Females within a colony of insects that are not able to reproduce. Their jobs may include feeding the queen, guarding the hive, maintaining the hive, collecting food or feeding the larvae. Most workers have one job throughout their short life span.

Index

Ant 6, 11, 12, 13, **38**, 62
Antenna 14, 41
Aphid 56, 60
Arachnid 11, 44, 54
Arthropod 11, 86
Backswimmer 6, **18**, 33
Bee 7, 11, 12, **70**
Beetles 11, 13, 36, 52, 60, 62
Butterfly 7, 11, 13, 15, **72-81, 92-93**
Caddisfly 6, 11, **20**, 28
Caterpillar 13,15, 66, 72
Centipede 6, 11,13, **40**, 52
Classification 11,15
Cricket 6, 11, **42**
Crustacean 11, 28, 52
Cuticle 14, 30, 45, 52
Daddy Longleg 6, 11, **44**, 55
Damselfly 6, 11, **22**
Decomposer 12, 28, 50
Dragonfly 6, 11, 13, **22**
Earthworm 7, 11, 12, 13, **46**
Earwig 7, 11, 13, **48**
Exoskeleton 14, 19, 86, 87
Gall Maker 56
Grasshopper 7, 11, 12, 43, **58**
Ladybug 7, 13, 14, **60**
Larva 15, 16, 86, 87
Mayfly 6, 11, 12, 21, **24,** 28, 29, 32
Metamorphosis 15, 16, 86-87
Millipede 7, 11, 12, 13, 40, **50**
Mollusk 11, 62
Molt 14, 24, 27, 45, 72, 86, 87
Mosquito 6, 11, 12, 15, 22, 25, **26,** 35
Moth 7, 11, 20, **82, 94**
Pupa 16, 82, 86, 87
Roly-poly 7, 11, 13, 12, 51, **52**
Scud 6, 11, 12, **28**

Slug 7, 11, **62**
Spider 7, 11, 44, **54**
Spittlebug 7, **64**
Stonefly 6, 11, 21, 28, 29, **30,** 32
Tent Caterpillar 7, **66**
Tick 7, 11, **68**
Wasp 7, 11, 12, **84**
Water Boatman 6, 19, **32**
Water Strider 6, 14, **34**
Whirligig Beetle 6, 19, **36**

References

BOOKS

Carle, Eric. *The Very Hungry Caterpillar*. Philomel Books. 1979.

Cranshaw, Whitney and B. Kondratieff. *Guide to Colorado Insects*. Westcliffe Publishers, Inc. 2006.

Cranshaw, Whitney S. *Garden Insects of North America: the Ultimate Backyard Guide to Backyard Bugs*. Princeton University Press. 2004.

Eaton, E.R. and K. Kaufman. *Field Guide to Insects of North America*. Houghton Mifflin Co. 2007.

Ehlert, Lois. *Feathers for Lunch*. Harcourt Brace Jovanovich. 1990.

Goor, Ron & Nancy. *Insect Metamorphosis From Egg to Adult*. Macmillan Publishing Company. 1990.

Opler, Paul. *A Field Guide to Western Butterflies, 2nd edition*.Houghton Mifflin Co. 1999.

Ward, James V., Boris C. Kondratieff, and Robert E. Zuellig. *An Illustrated Guide to the Mountain Stream Insects of Colorado, 2nd edition*. University Press of Colorado. 2002.

Wexo, John Bonnett. *Zoobooks Insects.* Wildlife Education Ltd. 1989.

WEBSITES

www.butterfliesandmoths.org
www.ipmimages.org
www.bugguide.net

ABOUT THE AUTHOR

Garrick taught environmental education at the Aspen Center for Environmental Studies (ACES) for four years, taught high school science in the African kingdom of Lesotho with the U.S. Peace Corps, taught elementary school at the Aspen Community School for three years and currently teaches middle school Language Arts. He continues to teach environmental education courses in the summer months. He lives with his wife, Lindsay, and their two sons in Basalt, CO.

ABOUT THE ILLUSTRATOR

Hilary is an artist, a naturalist, and an educator. Some of her earliest memories are of wearing smocks and painting at easels in pre-school in West Lafayette, IN. Her passion for the visual arts has been lifelong. She is an illustrator and mixed media artist who has worked in photography, oil painting, textiles, printmaking and papermaking. She sells enameled jewelry with bold colors and geometric designs. In addition, she works in the field of scientific illustration. Hilary has been an educator for the past ten years. With degrees in both biology and art education she has taught environmental education, guided adventure trips and taught visual arts at the K-12 level. She has been teaching art to K-8th grade students at the Aspen Communtiy School for six years. She also teaches at Anderson Ranch during the summer. Hilary lives in Basalt, CO.

OTHER BOOKS WRITTEN BY GARRICK PFAFFMANN & ILLUSTRATED BY HILARY FORSYTH INCLUDE

Family Field Guide Series Volume 1: Rocky Mountain Mammals
Family Field Guide Series Volume 2: Rocky Mountain Plants: Trees.Shrubs. Wildflowers
Family Field Guide Series Volume 3: Rocky Mountain Birds

family field guide

family field guide
— SERIES —

field notes

family field guide
— SERIES —

field notes

family field guide